A tender plant from the dry ground

A vision from Isaiah of the crucified Jesus

Timothy Cross

DayOne

Endorsements

In 20 short chapters, Cross takes us through the verses that are the high watermark of Old Testament prophecy, Isaiah 52:13 to 53:12. There are no pretensions to scholarliness or original thought in this devotional commentary. Each section is biblical (scripture references abound on every page), sermonic (usually three brief points), alliterative (every chapter begins with the letter S) and theologically Reformed; the style is plain and straightforward. Although A tender plant from the dry ground *can be read in a single sitting, the book is ideal for a month's daily readings for those young in the Christian faith and also for those not so young in the faith.*

When I was in the pastoral ministry, I once preached a series of evangelistic sermons on Isaiah 53. If Timothy Cross's volume had been available then, it would have helped me to arrange my material better, inspired me to further (and deeper) thought on some of the verses and would have probably doubled the length of the series.

Although A tender plant from the dry ground *is no substitute for heftier and more scholarly commentaries (nor does it pretend to be), it is, nevertheless, a helpful little volume that will be of use to everyone who reads it.*

— **Mike Moore, Christian Witness to Israel**

Isaiah 53 is one of the most remarkable chapters of the Bible. It is the Old Testament version of the New Testament gospel of Christ, and so could be used to present the gospel of the Lord Jesus Christ even to those who do not accept the divine inspiration of the New Testament Scriptures. This devotional exposition of Isaiah 53 by Dr Timothy Cross brings out something of the wonder of the Word of God and the glory of the Christ of God. In explaining Isaiah's verses, the author covers almost every facet of the person and work of the Lord Jesus Christ predicted so clearly by Isaiah in his prophecy centuries beforehand. I commend Dr Cross for this excellent work.

—**Dr. Cecil Johnson, President, Christian Bible College, Rocky Mount, North Carolina, USA**

© Day One Publications 2011

All scripture quotations, unless otherwise indicated, are taken from the New King James Version®. Copyright © 1982 by Thomas Nelson, Inc. Used by permission. All rights reserved.

British Library Cataloguing in Publication Data available

ISBN 978-1-84625-314-0

Published by Day One Publications
Ryelands Road, Leominster, HR6 8NZ

☎ 01568 613 740
FAX: 01568 611 473
email—sales@dayone.co.uk
web site—www.dayone.co.uk
North American e-mail—usasales@dayone.co.uk
North American web site—www.dayonebookstore.com

All rights reserved

No part of this publication may be reproduced, or stored in a retrieval system, or transmitted, in any form or by any means, mechanical, electronic, photocopying, recording or otherwise, without the prior permission of Day One Publications.

Designed by Wayne McMaster and printed by Orchard Press, Cheltenham Ltd.

Contents

Preface 6
Isaiah 53 8
1 The surprise 10
2 The start 18
3 The shape 26
4 The suffering 32
5 The sorrow 36
6 The substitute 42
7 The strays 48
8 The silence 54
9 The sheep 60
10 The stricken 66
11 The Scriptures 74
12 The sinlessness 80
13 The sovereignty 88
14 The sacrifice 94
15 The success 100
16 The satisfaction 108
17 The salvation 114
18 The sin-bearer 122
19 The song 128
20 The service 134
   Endnotes 142

Preface

Martin Luther once said that Isaiah 53 'ought to be written on parchment of gold and lettered in diamonds.' Isaiah 53 is truly one of the most remarkable chapters in the whole Bible. Although written some 700 years BC, it actually contains one of the clearest views of the Person and Work of Christ in all of the Scriptures. This ancient Old Testament prophecy gives us a distilled New Testament theology.

Isaiah 53 directs us to heart of the biblical revelation, as it directs us to the Cross of Christ and the Christ of the Cross. The central theme of Isaiah 53 is the sacrificial, substitutionary and saving death of the Lord Jesus Christ at Calvary, and the infinite blessings and benefits which accrue to the believer from this. The Lord Jesus Christ Himself had Isaiah 53 in mind when He stated: 'And truly the Son of Man goes as it has been determined ... For I say to you that this which is written must still be accomplished in Me: "'And He was numbered with the transgressors'" (Luke 22:22, 37).

Isaiah is justly known as 'the evangelical prophet', and Isaiah 53 encapsulates his 'evangel'. Isaiah 53 is really the 'Gospel according to Isaiah'. If we have grasped the message of Isaiah 53, we have grasped the message of the whole Bible, and if the blessing of Isaiah 53 is ours, we will be blessed indeed and eternally rich with 'the unsearchable riches of Christ'—GRACE—**G**od's **R**iches **A**t **C**hrist's **E**xpense.

Timothy Cross,
Cardiff, Wales

Preface

A tender plant from the dry ground

Isaiah 53

¹Who has believed our report?
  And to whom has the arm of the L ORD been revealed?
²For He shall grow up before Him as a tender plant,
  And as a root out of dry ground.
  He has no form or comeliness;
  And when we see Him,
  There is no beauty that we should desire Him.
³He is despised and rejected by men,
  A Man of sorrows and acquainted with grief.
  And we hid, as it were, our faces from Him;
  He was despised, and we did not esteem Him.
⁴Surely He has borne our griefs
  And carried our sorrows;
  Yet we esteemed Him stricken,
  Smitten by God, and afflicted.
⁵But He was wounded for our transgressions,
  He was bruised for our iniquities;
  The chastisement for our peace was upon Him,
  And by His stripes we are healed.
⁶All we like sheep have gone astray;
  We have turned, every one, to his own way;
  And the L ORD has laid on Him the iniquity of us all.
⁷He was oppressed and He was afflicted,
  Yet He opened not His mouth;
  He was led as a lamb to the slaughter,
  And as a sheep before its shearers is silent,

So He opened not His mouth.
⁸He was taken from prison and from judgment,
And who will declare His generation?
For He was cut off from the land of the living;
For the transgressions of My people He was stricken.
⁹And they made His grave with the wicked—
But with the rich at His death,
Because He had done no violence,
Nor was any deceit in His mouth.
¹⁰Yet it pleased the Lord to bruise Him;
He has put Him to grief.
When You make His soul an offering for sin,
He shall see His seed, He shall prolong His days,
And the pleasure of the Lord shall prosper in His hand.
¹¹He shall see the labor of His soul, and be satisfied.
By His knowledge My righteous Servant shall justify many,
For He shall bear their iniquities.
¹²Therefore I will divide Him a portion with the great,
And He shall divide the spoil with the strong,
Because He poured out His soul unto death,
And He was numbered with the transgressors,
And He bore the sin of many,
And made intercession for the transgressors.

The surprise

'*Who has believed our report? And to whom has the arm of the* Lord *been revealed?*'

Isaiah 53:1

The name 'Isaiah' means 'The Lord delivers' or 'The Lord saves'. Isaiah was predominantly a prophet and preacher of God's salvation. If we search the Bible, we see that the expression 'the arm of the Lord' in our verse is actually another synonym for God's salvation. To Moses, for instance, God made the promise: 'I am the Lord; I will bring you out from under the burdens of the Egyptians, I will rescue you from their bondage, and I will redeem you with *an outstretched arm* …' (Exodus 6:6, my emphasis). The nation of Israel soon rejoiced that God kept this promise. They celebrated how 'The Lord brought us out of Egypt with a mighty hand and with an *outstretched arm*' (Deuteronomy 26:8, my emphasis). Similarly, only a few verses previous to our verse, Isaiah prophesied in the prophetic past tense 'The Lord has made bare *His holy arm* in the eyes of all the nations; and all the ends of the earth shall see the salvation of our God'(Isaiah 52:10, my emphasis). The Hebrew parallelism used here shows that the Lord's 'holy arm' and God's 'salvation' are one and the same. To save His people, therefore, almighty God in mercy and grace figuratively 'rolls up His sleeves' and intervenes on their behalf.

The Problem of Unbelief

With such a thrilling message of salvation, intricately bound

A tender plant from the dry ground

up with the Servant who would bring this salvation about, we can understand Isaiah's surprise and perplexity at a less than favourable response to his message. 'Who has believed our report?' Every preacher of the gospel can no doubt relate to Isaiah's feelings. In Isaiah 49:4, during one of his darker days, in exasperated tones the prophet exclaimed, 'I have laboured in vain, I have spent my strength for nothing and in vain …' The greatest message—the gospel of God—is sometimes met with apathy and unbelief.

Isaiah's sad surprise, however, was not a unique experience. He actually stood in a noble line. Even the Saviour of whom Isaiah spoke knew what it was like to meet with unbelief, as well as repentance and saving faith. John concludes his account of the Lord Jesus' public ministry by employing our verse as an explanation: 'But although He had done so many signs before them, they did not believe in Him; that the word of Isaiah the prophet might be fulfilled, which he spoke: "Lord, who has believed our report, and to whom has the arm of the Lord been revealed?"' (John 12:37, 38). The apostle Paul also experienced a mixed response to his gospel ministrations as well. When he preached the gospel in Rome, Luke records 'some were persuaded by the things which were spoken, and some disbelieved' (Acts 28:24). Paul had already written in his Roman epistle 'But they have not all obeyed the gospel. For Isaiah says, "Lord, who has believed our report?"' (Romans 10:16).

Isaiah 53:1, therefore, brings us face to face with the

The surprise

problem of unbelief. Gospel preachers may well be in for an unwelcome surprise. Yes, the gospel of Christ is God's own provision and answer for our deepest, direst need. It is indeed the divine remedy for our human malady. Yet this remedy may be refused. The preached gospel may meet with unbelief, hostility, apathy or even outright rejection and scorn.

The reality of unbelief being what it is, the question is asked: Is all gospel endeavour pointless? Are all preachers doomed to fail? Is every preacher destined to say with Isaiah 'I have laboured in vain, I have spent my strength for nothing and in vain'? (Isaiah 49:4). The answer, according to the Bible, is a resounding 'No!' For the same Scriptures which tell of the problem of unbelief also tell of the sure and certain triumph of the gospel of God's grace. Almighty God can never be frustrated and thwarted in His eternal purpose to save His people and glorify His name. The unbelief of puny men is no barrier to omnipotence!

The Sure Triumph of the Gospel

'Who has believed our report?' was the perplexed question sighed by Isaiah. Acts 13:48 gives us the answer to Isaiah's question, when it describes how, in response to hearing the gospel 'as many as had been appointed to eternal life believed.' This verse shows that the act of believing which results in salvation, while a human act, actually has its ultimate cause in God's election, that is, His eternal choice of some for eternal life. It is those who have been chosen by God in eternity past who will most certainly believe in Christ in time. God Himself sees to this, for saving faith is a gift which He Himself bestows in His sovereign grace. Salvation is wholly and solely a work of God. It is He alone who can open blind eyes, soften hard hearts, convict of sin, break down the barrier of unbelief, draw to the foot of the cross and bestow saving faith in Christ.

The Golden Chain of God's Salvation

The full answer to Isaiah's question concerning believing and experiencing the arm of the LORD in salvation is given us in Romans 8:30. This a compact verse summarizing the whole 'sweep' of salvation from eternity past to eternity future. The verse gives us a remarkable insight into the divine scheme and economy. Romans 8:30 states:

'Moreover whom He predestined, these He also called; whom He called these He also justified; and whom He justified, these He also glorified.'

This compact, summary verse informs us that salvation is a result of four works of God—four golden links in an unbreakable chain. The four links are these: (a) Predestination (b) Vocation (c) Justification and (d) Glorification.

(a) Predestination

'Whom He predestined ...' According to the Bible, we believe in Christ because we have been predestined by God so to do. The Bible teaches divine election. Divine election refers to God's prerogative in choosing whom He wills for eternal blessing in Christ. 'He chose us in Him before the foundation of the world' (Ephesians 1:4).

(B) VOCATION

'Whom He predestined, these He also called ...' Those chosen by God in eternity past will most certainly hear the call of the gospel in time, and be enabled to respond to it. The technical term for this is 'effectual calling.' The *Shorter Catechism* defines it this way: 'Effectual calling is the work of God's Spirit, whereby convincing us of our sin and misery, enlightening our minds in the knowledge of Christ and renewing our wills He doth persuade and enable us to embrace Jesus Christ, freely offered to us in the gospel' [1] (Q. 31). Put poetically, 'He drew me and I followed on, charmed to confess the voice divine.' It is through the preaching of the gospel that God calls and draws sinners to Himself.

(C) JUSTIFICATION

'Whom He called, these He also justified ...' Once the sinner has been effectually drawn to Christ, the most remarkable, eternal transaction occurs. God declares the guilty sinner 'Not guilty' for Christ's sake. By virtue of the sinless Saviour's death on the cross, guilty sinners may go free. The *Shorter Catechism* again states, 'Justification is an act of God's free grace wherein He pardoneth all our sins and accepteth us as righteous in His sight, only for the righteousness of Christ imputed to us and received by faith alone'.[2]

The final link in God's golden chain of salvation, according to Romans 8:30, is that of

(d) Glorification

'Whom He justified, these He also glorified.' Glorification is, of course, future, and yet the verb here is in the past tense. It shows that in the sight of God it is a 'fait accompli'. Glorification is the consummation of God's redemptive purpose for His people. Salvation has a goal. The goal is glorification.

We see, then, from the golden chain of God's salvation that there is a wonderful harmony and order about God's ways of grace. Scripture enables us to trace His redemptive process: He elects sinners in Christ; He sent His Son to die to procure the salvation of the same; He sends His Spirit to accompany the preaching of His Word to draw these people to Christ and believe in Him; God then preserves these, in Christ, for eternal life. God's salvation, then, has election at one end and glorification at the other. His purposes of grace have been planned in eternity, accomplished in time both by Christ and in the earthly experience of His elect, and will be consummated and climaxed in eternity to come in the ultimate glorification of His people, when 'They shall see His face' (Revelation 22:4) and be saved to sin no more.

Unbelief?

'Who has believed our report and to whom has the arm of the LORD been revealed?' (Isaiah 53:1). On this seemingly negative note, Isaiah 53 opens. The prophet Isaiah, in common with most preachers of the gospel, was surprised and perplexed at the response—or lack of it—to his message. Preachers, however, are called to be faithful, not necessarily successful by this world's measure. The God of the Bible is a sovereign God. Appearances to the contrary, He will most certainly accomplish the salvation of His people. Nothing can hinder or frustrate the Almighty from fulfilling His purposes of grace. 'The LORD of hosts has sworn, saying: "Surely as I have thought, so it shall come to pass, and as I have purposed, so it shall stand"' (Isaiah 14:24). 'Your God reigns' (Isaiah 52:7).

Reflect on these points

1. Is divine election a disincentive or an incentive for evangelistic endeavour?

2. What is the Christian way to react when our Christian testimony is met with apathy, hostility or ridicule?

3. Considering that preaching is so central in the divine economy in relation to accomplishing God's eternal purposes of grace, do you pray regularly for preachers of the gospel and the preaching of the gospel?

The start

'For He shall grow up before Him as a tender plant, and as a root out of dry ground.'

Isaiah 53:2

The One of whom Isaiah spoke in His matchless prophecy actually had no start. The Servant of the Lord had always existed, and existed while Isaiah prophesied, even though his prophecy referred to a ministry which the Servant would undertake some seven centuries in the future. The One of whom Isaiah spoke had no beginning—He was as eternal as God Himself is eternal.

Yet, the One of whom Isaiah spoke, paradoxically, also did have a beginning, for at a particular moment in time and space, God became man and was born as a baby in Bethlehem, and then grew up to mature manhood. The incarnation is one of the major milestones in the story of redemption. 'In the beginning was the Word, and the Word was with God, and the Word was God ... And the Word became flesh and dwelt among us ...'(John 1:14):

The Servant's Humble Origins

'For He shall grow up before Him as a young plant ...' Isaiah here seems to be referring to what were, humanly speaking, the humble origins and early years of the human life of the One who is the eternal Son of God. The Gospel records actually devote relatively little space to this period, their focus being—in line with Isaiah's prophecy—on the death of Christ, as opposed to His life. Luke, however, records that the Lord Jesus 'grew

A tender plant from the dry ground

up'. 'And Jesus increased in wisdom and stature, and in favour with God and men' (Luke 2:52). Christ's humanity, then, was normal, albeit sinless.

Humanly speaking, Christ's earthly roots were humble ones. His earthly father, Joseph, was a carpenter by trade, and the Lord Jesus, as was customary, followed in Joseph's footsteps until the time for His public ministry began, when He was about thirty years old. 'Is this not the carpenter, the Son of Mary …?' (Mark 6:3).

Christ grew up in a humble town—the town of Nazareth in northern Israel. Nazareth is not mentioned in the Old Testament at all, and the town would no doubt have remained in obscurity had not the Lord Jesus 'put it on the map'. That Nazareth was not particularly highly esteemed is evident from Nathaniel's remark 'Can anything good come out of Nazareth?' (John 1:46).

Isaiah thus relates the humanly humble beginnings of the One who was to come. 'For He shall grow up before Him as a young plant.' But Isaiah expands, and also speaks of Him as being 'as a root out of dry ground' too. Isaiah is keen to balance the Servant's meekness with His majesty.

The Root

Isaiah had already prophesied of the coming One using this term. In Isaiah 11:1 f. he states 'There shall come forth a Rod from the stump of Jesse, and a Branch shall grow out of his roots. The Spirit of the LORD shall rest upon Him …'

David—Jesse's son—was Israel's greatest earthly king. The

Jews looked back to David's reign as something of a golden age. Understandably, then, when they looked forward to the coming of the Messiah, they interpreted it through 'Davidic spectacles'. The Messiah would be of David's line. With the coming of Christ, these Messianic hopes and aspirations were superabundantly realized. Jesus was indeed born of David's line of descendants—'born of the seed of David according to the flesh' (Romans 1:3). Matthew opens his Gospel by recording Christ's human genealogy so: 'The book of the genealogy of Jesus Christ, the Son of David …' (Matthew 1:1). King David was, of course, a great king—yet his flaws and character blemishes are all too evident from the pages of Scripture, too. Jesus, however, is described in the Bible as the King of kings. He is 'Great David's Greater Son'—the supreme, supernal and sinless Son of God. As the eternal Son of God, paradoxically, Christ both preceded and succeeded King David, hence the risen, ascended and glorified Christ's assertion in Revelation 22:16: 'I am the root and offspring of David.'

The Virgin Birth of Christ

Isaiah's prophecy concerning the coming Servant's early days is most unusual in that it describes Him 'as a root out of dry ground.' Elementary biology teaches us that this is impossible. A root cannot grow without moisture, for water is essential for life. Isaiah is thus hinting that the Servant's beginnings on earth would be miraculous, that is, beyond what would normally be humanly possible. Isaiah is thus pointing us to the 'virgin birth', that is, the virginal conception of Christ.

A tender plant from the dry ground

As a root cannot normally grow out of dry ground, likewise a child cannot normally be conceived without the agency of a human father. Isaiah, though, unusually prophesied that the coming Servant would be 'as a root out of dry ground.' He prophesied that the Servant's birth would be miraculous.

Earlier on in Isaiah 7:14, Isaiah both foretold and forth told: 'Behold, the virgin shall conceive and bear a Son, and shall call His name Immanuel.' His prophecy has just one fulfillment: In the miraculous conception of the Lord Jesus Christ. He was as the Apostles' Creed states, 'conceived by the Holy Ghost and born of the Virgin Mary.' Christ was conceived without the agency of a human father. God was His Father. Mary, Christ's mother, was initially—and understandably—very puzzled as to how she could possibly conceive a child without the instrumentality of a human male. The angel from heaven thus explained to her how: 'The Holy Spirit will come upon you, and the power of the Highest will overshadow you, therefore, also, that Holy One Who is to be born will be called the Son of God' (Luke 1:35). Matthew similarly records that Christ's conception was 'that it might be fulfilled which was spoken by the Lord through the prophet, saying: "Behold, a virgin shall be with child, and bear a Son, and they shall call His name Immanuel" which is translated "God with us."' (Matthew 1:22, 23).

The Necessity of the Virgin Birth
Even a cursory reading of the Bible then reveals that Christ's conception was a miraculous one. He was indeed *a root out*

of dry ground. He was born of a virgin. The 'virgin birth' of Christ is actually one of the fundamentals of the Christian faith. Only a sinless One can redeem sinners. Had Christ had a human father, He would have inherited our sinful human nature, for all those born of Adam have a sin-tainted nature. We are sinners by nature and by practice. Christ's sinlessness and His virgin birth are inextricably bound. It was by the virgin birth that the eternal entered into time and God became man. Christ did not inherit Adam's sinful nature, and, being sinless, was able to offer Himself up as a perfect sacrifice on behalf of sinners— 'as of a lamb without blemish and without spot' (1 Peter 1:19). Isaiah's stress on the efficacy of the Servant's suffering is invalidated if the Servant Himself was a sinner. The Servant, however, had no sinful nature because He was supernaturally conceived through the instrumentality of God the Holy Spirit.

The Glory of the One Virgin Born

And so we note the Servant's start in life, as prophesied by Isaiah. 'He shall grow up before Him as a tender plant and as a root out of dry ground.' The Christ of the Bible had no origins. He is eternal—'Whose origin is from of old, from everlasting' (Micah 5:2, KJV). Yet at a moment in time, in Christ, God became man and was 'conceived by the power of the Holy Spirit and born of the Virgin Mary'. Christ's birth was a miraculous birth. It was 'as a root out of dry ground'—a work of God Himself, beyond human resource and ability.

A tender plant from the dry ground

Reflect on these points

1. *Considering the humility of Christ, is humility a neglected Christian virtue? Why has every Christian cause to be humble?*
2. *Why is Christ's virgin birth one of the non-negotiable doctrines of the Christian faith?*
3. *How would you reply to the Jehovah's Witnesses when they purport that Christ was not eternal but came into being in time? Why is Christ's eternality so essential?*

The start

The shape

'He has no form or comeliness; and when we see Him, there is no beauty that we should desire Him.'

Isaiah 53:2

In our verse here, Isaiah prophesies that, as far as outward appearances are concerned, there would be nothing particularly remarkable about the coming Servant of the Lord.

The Graeco-Roman world into which the coming Christ was born prized physical beauty. (It is the Greeks who bequeathed to us the Olympic Games.) It would seem though that, as far as external beauty goes, Christ was not the most handsome man on earth, if it is permissible to say so. Of course, we have no way of verifying Isaiah's prophecy, because the Gospel records are silent as regards Christ's physical appearance, and the Bible forbids graven images, that is, visible depictions of the deity.

As part of the inerrant Word of God, however, we believe that what Isaiah prophesied is completely true. While we may surmise that Christ would have looked Middle Eastern—with the distinctive, olive-coloured skin of that region, and wearing the distinctive clothes peculiar to first century Israel—the Holy Spirit has not seen fit to give us a physical description of the Saviour. We may speculate that this is to prevent the danger of idolatry and graven images. What would have happened, for instance, if Christ had had His portrait painted? What would have happened had photography existed in the first century? We shudder to think … The only physical memorial of Christ

A tender plant from the dry ground

which has the divine mandate is perishable bread and wine, objects which can hardly be venerated.

Isaiah thus prophesied that the coming Servant of the Lord would possess neither 'star athlete' shape nor 'film star' looks. Such is another pointer that His prophecy is of God and not man. Surely Isaiah 53:2 would have been completely opposite had this prophecy stemmed from Isaiah's own mind and creative devices. Isaiah's prophecy, though, is divine and not human, 'for prophecy never came by the will of man, but holy men of God spoke as they were moved by the Holy Spirit' (2 Peter 1:21).

Going beyond the external

According to the Bible, outward appearances can deceive. Proverbs 31:30 tells us that 'Charm is deceitful, and beauty is vain.' Pertinently, 1 Samuel 16:7 informs us that 'the LORD does not see as man sees; for man looks at the outward appearance, but the LORD looks at the heart.'

Christ's external appearance was also deceptive. Yes, as regards His outward appearance, He may not have seemed particularly handsome or particularly distinguishable from any other young male walking around the Israel of His day. But this does not detract from the fact that Christ, while human, is no mere man. The Bible affirms that 'In Him dwells all the whole fullness of the Godhead bodily' (Colossians 2:9) and 'Great is the mystery of godliness: God was manifested in the flesh' (1 Timothy 3:16). It has been well written:

His appearance afforded no clue to His identity. He looked like a young Galilean peasant, an artisan from northern Palestine. Only a divine revelation can unfold to men the truth about this lowly One, that in Him dwells all the fullness of the Godhead bodily, that in Him are hid all the treasures of wisdom and knowledge, that He is the image of the invisible God, the firstborn of all creation, the outshining of God's glory, the express image of His person, the Son of God become the Son of man, from everlasting to everlasting.[1]

Who do you say that I am?

In 2 Corinthians 5:16 Paul explained 'though we have known Christ according to the flesh (that is, from a human point of view), yet now we know Him thus no longer.' A right view of Christ is impossible apart from a supernatural operation of the Holy Spirit in the human heart and mind, revealing His true identity to us. Christ can only be truly understood if the Holy Spirit imparts a true spiritual discernment of Him to us. The 'natural man'—one who is unconverted and devoid of the Holy Spirit—may indeed admire Christ as a teacher, miracle worker, a 'good' man or even as a martyr. The natural man—unaware of his need for a Saviour—will most likely see nothing special or supernatural about Christ at all. 'He has no form or comeliness; and when we see Him, there is no beauty that we should desire Him.'

The Christian, however, will have no hesitation or

embarrassment in describing Christ as 'chief among ten thousand … and … altogether lovely' (Song of Solomon 5:10, 16). Christ's true 'beauty' is spiritually discerned. Enlightened by the Holy Spirit, the Christian is able to look beyond the unremarkable, outward appearance of Christ as mentioned by Isaiah in our title verse. The Christian uses language about Christ which the world would see as extravagant. Joining in with the worship of the Church militant on earth and triumphant in heaven, the Christian sings:

> The glorious company of the Apostles praise Thee
> The goodly fellowship of the prophets praise Thee
> The noble army of martyrs praise Thee
> The holy church throughout all the
> world doth acknowledge Thee
> THOU ART THE KING OF GLORY, O CHRIST
> THOU ART THE EVERLASTING
> SON OF THE FATHER. [2]

The shape

Reflect on these points

1. *'The* LORD *does not see as man sees; for man looks at the outward appearance, but the* LORD *looks at the heart' (1 Samuel 16:7). Ask yourself: 'Am I more concerned with the image I project outwardly to others, than with the state of my inner soul before God?'*
2. *Can you think of a time when you realized that 'appearances deceive' and that God's ways are not always our ways? (Look up 1 Corinthians 1:26 f.)*
3. *What does it take to have a full-orbed, biblical view of the Person of Christ? (c.f. Matthew 16:17)*

The suffering

> 'He is despised and rejected by men; a man of sorrows and acquainted with grief. And we hid, as it were, our faces from Him; He was despised, and we did not esteem Him.'
>
> ***Isaiah 53:3***

Isaiah foresaw and prophesied that the coming 'Suffering Servant' of the Lord would experience suffering in all its forms. With our New Testament hindsight, we know that the Christ who came did indeed experience the most excruciating suffering, in both His life and His death. Our Saviour knows what it is like to suffer.

The Saviour's Rejection

The experience of rejection is a particularly cruel form of suffering, even though its wounds are psychological rather than physical. Hebrews 13:12 tells us that 'Jesus also, that He might sanctify the people with His own blood, suffered outside the gate.' The Saviour knew rejection—a rejection which culminated in people shouting, 'Crucify Him' and His being crucified outside the walls of Jerusalem, where He underwent the rejection of men and even the turning away of the face of God the Father Himself.

When Jesus bore the sins of His people, God the Father turned away from Him. Sin is anathema to God's holy nature, hence the sin-bearer cried out in agony, 'My God, My God, why have You forsaken Me?' (Matthew 27:46).

When we think of Christ as being 'despised and rejected by men' naturally our thoughts gravitate to Calvary—Calvary

A tender plant from the dry ground

being the ultimate in human despicability and rejection. The rejection of Christ, though, while culminating at Calvary, was not confined to that place.

John 1:11 tells us that Christ 'came to His own and His own did not receive Him.' Luke 4:29 describes how the citizens of Nazareth—Jesus' home town—once 'rose up and thrust Him out of the city, and they led Him to the brow of the hill on which their city was built, that they might throw Him down over the cliff.' Isaiah's prediction came true. 'He is despised and rejected by men.' Christ knew the scorn and contempt of the enemy and the irrational rejection of those who, humanly speaking, should have been His friends. 'But I am a worm and no man; a reproach of men and despised of the people' (Psalm 22:6). So the Saviour knew the peculiar and particular suffering which is rejection.

The Saviour's Sympathy

The Saviour's experience of rejection reinforces the truth of Hebrews 4:15, that in Christ we have a sympathetic Saviour. His sympathy knows no bounds because His suffering knew no bounds. Hebrews 4:15 states: 'For we do not have a high priest who cannot sympathize with our weaknesses, but was in all points tempted as we are, yet without sin.'

Have you ever seen a statue of the Buddha? The Buddha is an idol—a god of stone who sits perched up on high, with a slight smirk upon his face. The facial expression is that of one seemingly far above and removed from the pain and suffering of life here on earth. The true God, however, is just not like that at all. The God of the Bible actually became man. He shared our human frame, sin apart. God in Christ knew suffering in its physical, psychological and spiritual forms. 'He is despised and rejected by men ...' God in Christ is thus able to sympathize with us in our suffering. Jesus understands! None of our depths will ever be as deep as those He has already plumbed. God in Christ is able to sympathize with us. And God in Christ is able to minister His all-sufficient grace to us, until the new Day breaks 'and sorrow and sighing shall flee away' (Isaiah 35:10).

Reflect on these points

1. *Considering that Christians worship a Saviour who knew rejection, should Christians expect to be popular?*
2. *How have you coped (or how would you cope) with the painful experience of personal rejection? (Look up Romans 8:31 f.).*
3. *What comfort can you draw from (a) Christ's rejection by men (b) Christ's being forsaken at Calvary by God?*

The sorrow

'He is despised and rejected by men, a man of sorrows and acquainted with grief. And we hid, as it were, our faces from Him; He was despised, and we did not esteem Him.'

Isaiah 53:3

It was this verse from Isaiah 53 which prompted Philipp Bliss to pen one of the English-speaking world's most well loved hymns:

> Man of sorrows!' What a name
> For the Son of God who came
> Ruined sinners to reclaim
> Hallelujah! What a Saviour!

Isaiah thus foretold a Messiah who would be 'a man of sorrows and acquainted with grief.' When we considered the suffering of Christ in the previous chapter, we saw that while the suffering of Christ climaxed at the cross, it was not confined to that place. It is the same now as we consider Christ's sorrow. While Christ's sorrow reached its peak when He was hung up to die on the cross, His sorrow was not limited to Calvary, for Christ experienced sorrow throughout His earthly ministry. The whole of Christ's ministry was characterized by intense sympathy and infinite sensitivity to the suffering and sorrow of others. Elsewhere, Isaiah said of the coming Servant that 'a bruised reed He will not break, and smoking flax He will not quench' (Isaiah 42:3).

The Servant's Humane Humanity

Isaiah foretells the Suffering Servant to be '*a **man** of* *sorrows.'* It is another reminder of the reality of the humanity of Christ. He really did share our human nature, sin apart. Sorrow is an intensely human condition. Animals do not weep and sympathize—neither do statues or computers. The incarnation is one of the fundamentals of the Christian faith, and one of the major milestones in the events of redemption. In Christ, God became man. He became man because immortal deity cannot die. In Christ, God became man so that He could pay the wages of human sin which is death. The humanity of Christ, then, is as real and undeniable as His deity. 'Inasmuch then as the children have partaken of flesh and blood, He Himself likewise shared in the same, that through death He might destroy him who had the power of death, that is, the devil'(Hebrews 2:14). The Shorter Catechism states:

> The only Redeemer of God's elect is the Lord Jesus Christ who, being the eternal Son of God became man, and so was and continueth to be, God and man in two distinct natures and one person for ever …

> Christ the Son of God became man by taking to Himself a true body and a reasonable soul, being conceived by the power of the Holy Ghost in the womb of the virgin Mary and born of her, yet without sin.[1]

The Sorrowful Saviour

'He is … a man of sorrows and acquainted with grief …' The shortest verse of the New Testament reads simply and succinctly: 'Jesus wept' (John 11:35). The context of this verse is the death—and subsequent raising to life again by Jesus—of Lazarus. Lazarus had two sisters, Martha and Mary. Naturally, they were devastated and grief-stricken by the death of their brother. The Lord Jesus identified with their grief and wept with them. The Lord Jesus also identified with the root and ultimate cause of their grief.

According to the Bible death—in its physical, spiritual and eternal manifestations—is God's judgment on sin. If there was no sin there would be no death and corruption. 'Through one man sin entered the world, and death through sin, and thus death spread to all men, because all sinned' (Romans 5:12). The Lord Jesus did more than sympathize with Martha and Mary's grief, and the ravages which sin had brought. He eradicated it! He went and raised Lazarus from the dead! Similarly, the Lord Jesus showed far more than a merely theoretical concern and sorrow at the human predicament of sin and death. He went on to save us by dying for our sins at Calvary. 'Christ died for our sins' (1 Corinthians 15:3). Because of the death and resurrection of Jesus, the Christian is able and will be able to shout the acclamation 'O Death, where is your sting? O Hades, where is your victory? The sting of death is sin, and the strength of sin is the law. But thanks be to God, Who gives us the victory through our Lord Jesus Christ' (1 Corinthians 15:55, 56).

The Man of Sorrows

The Lord Jesus, then, was 'a man of sorrows and acquainted

with grief' throughout His earthly life. He was always inwardly moved by the plight and need of others.

Consider a certain funeral which occurred once in the village of Nain. Here is a widow who is carrying out her only son. He is lying dead on a bier. Her hope of physical and emotional support in life has been taken away from her completely. But Luke records how 'When the Lord saw her, He had compassion on her and said to her "Do not weep"'(Luke 7:13). There followed another miracle. The Lord raised a dead person to life yet again …

Matthew 14:14 records 'When Jesus went out He saw a great multitude; and He was moved with compassion for them, and healed their sick.'

Consider Jesus' own words in Mark 8:2: 'I have compassion on the multitude …'—a compassion which resulted in the Lord employing His miraculous powers to feed that hungry multitude.

Luke 19:41 records at the commencement of the last week of the Lord's earthly ministry: 'Now as He drew near, He saw the city and *wept* over it, saying, "If you had known, even you, especially in this your day, the things that make for your peace!"'

Truly, of the Saviour it is well said: 'Grief was His intimate acquaintance; for He acquainted Himself with the grievances of others and sympathized with them.'[2]

The Sorrow of the Cross

While the life of Christ was characterized by sorrow, His

sorrow was to reach a climax in His death—that death which was the very reason for His coming into the world. Both the suffering and the sorrow of Christ reached their culmination in His cruel death on the cross, when He suffered and sorrowed for the sins of others. Writing prophetically of this—and putting words into the Saviour's mouth—another prophet, Jeremiah, wrote: 'Is it nothing to you, all you who pass by? Behold and see if there is any sorrow like My sorrow which has been brought on Me, which the LORD has inflicted on Me in the day of His fierce anger' (Lamentations 1:12).

It is to the death of the Servant that we will next turn in Isaiah's central stanza—central in every sense of the word. Isaiah, as the evangelical prophet, along with Paul, could also say 'we preach Christ crucified' (1 Corinthians 1:23), as we shall see in our next chapter.

Reflect on these points

1. *Why is it as essential to hold to Christ's humanity as it is to His deity?*
2. *List some Scriptures which reveal the true, tender humanity of Christ.*
3. *The Saviour knew sorrow, and His followers will also know sorrow. What is the Christian perspective on sorrow? Ponder Romans 8:18 and Revelation 21:4.*

The substitute

*'Surely He has borne our griefs and carried our sorrows; yet we esteemed Him stricken, smitten by God, and afflicted. But He was wounded for our transgressions, He was bruised for our iniquities; the chastisement for our peace was upon Him, and by His stripes we are healed. All we like sheep have gone astray; we have turned, every one, to his own way; and the L*ORD *has laid on Him the iniquity of us all.'*

Isaiah 53:4–6

Isaiah 53:4–6 is the central stanza of Isaiah's prophecy concerning the Suffering Servant who was to come. It is preceded by six verses and followed by six verses. The centrality of Isaiah 53:4–6 though is more than a matter of mathematics. These verses are central in every sense. They give us perhaps the clearest explanation of Calvary in the whole Bible, and in the Bible, all roads lead to Calvary. In the Bible, Calvary is central and literally crucial. The centre cross of Calvary is the heart and core of the message of the Bible and the Christian gospel.

John relates that the most momentous event of all occurred at 'a place called the place of a skull, which is called in Hebrew Golgotha, where they crucified Him (the Lord Jesus), and two others with Him, one on either side, and Jesus in the center' (John 19:17, 18).

The earliest ever statement of the Christian faith—a statement which sought to capture the very essence of the Christian gospel—states succinctly 'that Christ died for our sins according to the Scriptures' (1 Corinthians 15:3).

Isaiah's verses here depict Christ suffering as the sinner's substitute. He was stricken and smitten, not for His own sins but for the sins of others. (Verse 5 is the inspired commentary on verse 4).

Isaiah 53:4–6 then takes us to the absolute heart of the message of the Bible. 'He was wounded for our transgressions ...' Tomes have been written about them. Thousands of sermons have been preached explaining them, and thousands of hymns have been sung extolling them.

In Another's Stead

The dictionary defines a substitute as 'a person ... acting or serving in the place of another.' Isaiah's verses here are transparent when they state that the Servant was acting in the place of others. He was suffering not for His own sins, for in actual fact He had no sins for which He deserved to be punished. Rather, He was suffering for the sins of others. Isaiah states that Christ was acting on our behalf. He was suffering dreadfully so that we might escape from dreadful suffering. His suffering was thus 'vicarious'—it was in our room and stead. 'Surely He has borne *our* griefs and carried *our* sorrows ... He was wounded for *our* transgressions, He was bruised for *our* iniquities ... the LORD has laid on Him the iniquity of *us* all' (emphasis mine).

To transgress is to infringe the law. It is to overstep a limit laid down by God—to do something which He has expressly forbidden. Transgression against an eternal God merits eternal punishment. Transgression has to be paid for. Isaiah's gospel though tells the sinner how he may escape from paying transgressions' dreadful penalty. There is a way of deliverance because Christ paid the penalty for our transgressions in our stead—'for' us. 'He was wounded for *our* transgressions …'

Sin is an affront to God's holy nature. Sin evokes God's wrath. A holy God is at enmity with sinners. Sinners deserve God's eternal chastisement. But Isaiah's gospel proclaims that Christ was 'chastised' in our place. He bore the punishment which we deserve for our sins. Hence 'the chastisement for our peace was upon Him', for when we believe in the Saviour-substitute, our sins are forgiven, God's wrath is averted and we have peace with our Maker. John wrote of Christ, 'He Himself is the propitiation for our sins' (1 John 2:2). Paradoxically, 'by His stripes we are healed'— for it was His punishment that procured our pardon.

And so Isaiah vividly depicts the coming Christ as our Saviour-substitute. He died in our place. He was punished so that we might be pardoned. He was judged so that we might be justified. At Calvary, the sinless Christ took the place of sinners. At Calvary, to procure our salvation, Christ dealt with 'our transgressions … our iniquities …' for 'the LORD has laid on Him the iniquity of us all. '

Old Testament or New?

Isaiah's Old Testament prophecy dovetails with New Testament theology exactly. It is the Saviour-substitute Who unifies both Testaments. In this we see that the message of the Bible is one, and that the Bible has one sole Author, in spite of

A tender plant from the dry ground

its varied human authorship, separated by centuries of time. Let us see briefly that this is so.

As we have already seen, the earliest Christian creed states that 'Christ died for our sins' (1 Corinthians 15:3). Paul, in Romans 4:25, states that Christ 'was delivered up because of our offences' and in Romans 5:6 states that 'Christ died for the ungodly.' In Galatians 3:13 he says that 'Christ has redeemed us from the curse of the law having become a curse for us—for it is written "Cursed is every one who hangs on a tree."' In later years Peter—an apostle who in the days of Christ's life on earth was rather confused as to the meaning of the cross—stated with the hindsight of Christian maturity that Christ 'Himself bore our sins in His own body on the tree' (1 Peter 2:24) and that 'Christ also suffered once for sins, the just for the unjust' (1 Peter 3:18).

Christ's death on the cross as the sinner's substitute then could not be more central to the message of the Bible and the Christian gospel. Christ as sin-bearer—taking our sin and punishment upon Himself at Calvary—is the key which unlocks the whole Bible.

The absolutely crucial nature of Christ's vicarious sufferings in relation to the sinner's salvation is explained well in the following lines. Speaking of the darkness and dereliction of Calvary, along with Christ's anguished cry of 'My God my God, why have You forsaken Me?', John Keddie writes that at Calvary:

> [Christ] was undergoing God's judgment in the place of His people ... as we view the cross and hear this cry of agony and anguish uttered by the Lord at the height of

His sufferings, the truth must come home with power to our souls—either our sins are punished in Jesus for us, or we have to bear the punishment ourselves ...

All who will not have Christ—who refuse or ignore His claim upon them—will be exposed to the full punishment due justly for their sins. For they have no sin-bearer; they have not come under the shelter of His atonement. But for the believer, here is the truth: He was forsaken for me![1]

Under the inspiration of the Holy Spirit, then, Isaiah focuses on the Christ of Calvary. He was enabled to see Christ dying as the sinner's substitute. He was given the most vivid vision of the crucified Saviour who was to come. He saw the Christ of the cross and was enabled to understand and share the true meaning of the cross of Christ. He died, not for His own sins, but for the sins of others. The incomparable prophecy directs us to the incomparable Substitute.

Reflect on these points

1. *Why is it less than biblical to admire Christ solely as a teacher, miracle worker or good example?*
2. *Read Galatians 6:14. Everyone glories in something or someone. Do you know what it is to truly glory in the cross of Christ over and above everything else?*
3. *How would you go about explaining the substitutionary nature of Christ's death to an interested friend who has no Christian background?*

The strays

'*All we like sheep have gone astray, we have turned, every one, to his own way, and the* LORD *has laid on Him the iniquity of us all.*'

Isaiah 53:6

Sinful Strays

Although he is employing picture language, in the verse above Isaiah gives us a realistic and honest description of the human condition and nature apart from the grace of God. 'All we like sheep have gone astray, we have turned, every one, to his own way.' The apostle Paul says the same when he gives the diagnosis of the sinful human condition in Romans 3:11, 12. This, he concludes, includes the fact that 'there is none who seeks for God. They have all gone out of the way …'

We are, Isaiah says, like stray sheep. A stray sheep is a pitiful creature. It is away from the warmth and safety of the fold and out of the reach of the shepherd's care. It is exposed to the elements and at the mercy of wild beasts stronger than itself. It is separated from where it should and ought to be.

Our sinful condition has many parallels with a stray, irrational, self-willed sheep. Sin separates us from the Shepherd. The Bible pictures God Himself as a Shepherd many times. 'The LORD is my shepherd' (Psalm 23:1). Isaiah had already used the metaphor in Isaiah 40:11 where we read 'He (God) will feed His flock like a shepherd; He will gather the lambs with His arm, and carry them in His bosom, and gently

A tender plant from the dry ground

lead those who are with young.' Sin, however, cuts us off from the Shepherd, for a holy God can have nothing to do with sin. 'Your iniquities have separated you from your God; and your sins have hidden His face from you so that He will not hear' (Isaiah 59:2).

By nature, then, we go our own way and not God's. We go astray, turn away from our Maker and 'do our own thing', thus rendering ourselves liable to the greatest danger of all, namely exposing ourselves to the eternal wrath of God. He is righteously indignant against all those who rebel against Him and flout His law. 'All we like sheep have gone astray; we have turned every one to his own way …' We thus desperately need to be rescued and we need to be reconciled.

Saved Sheep

Isaiah 53:6 not only gives the diagnosis of the human condition but it also gives the needed remedy. The verse contains a terrible indictment, but it also tells of the way of deliverance which God has provided. This glad and welcome news comes from the fact that 'The LORD has laid on Him the iniquity of us all.' That is, the very cause of our separation—our sin—has been dealt with by God in His mercy. Isaiah no doubt had the Day of Atonement in mind when he uttered this prophesy. On the Day of Atonement the sin of the people was, symbolically, transferred to a 'scapegoat' and carried away. Leviticus 16:21f. gives the details: 'Aaron shall lay both his hands on the head of the live goat and confess over it all the iniquities of the children of Israel, and all their transgressions, concerning all their sins

… putting them on the *head of the* goat and shall send it away into the wilderness … The goat shall bear on itself all their iniquities to an uninhabited land …'

Yet with our New Testament hindsight, we can see that Isaiah was surely speaking of the Christ to come, for the New Testament is adamant that 'The LORD has laid on Him the iniquity of us all.' That is, Christ, as we have seen, was made liable for the sins of others—for our sins: 'Who Himself bore our sins in His own body on the tree' (1 Peter 2:24).

'Christ was offered once to bear the sins of many' (Hebrews 9:28). And in one of the most profound statements in the whole Bible, Paul states that:

'For He made Him who knew no sin to be sin for us, that we might become the righteousness of God in Him' (2 Corinthians 5:21), that is, the sinless Christ took upon Himself our sin and guilt so that we might be declared 'not guilty' and have our relationship with God repaired.

The gospel according to Isaiah, then, is that those sins which separate us from God and damn our souls can be transferred to Another. They can be dealt with and put away by Christ. The Christian's glad testimony is 'He bore all my sins on Calvary's cross.'

The Safety of the Fold
We have seen that our sinful condition makes us akin to a lost, stray sheep. Sin separates us from the warmth of the fold and fellowship with the Shepherd. We have also seen that God, in Christ, in infinite mercy, has taken a gracious initiative to deal

with the sin which separates us from Him. 'The LORD has laid on Him the iniquity of us all.' All this being so, it comes as no surprise to see that the Bible pictures salvation as a returning to the safety of the fold. Salvation involves being rescued by the Shepherd, returning to God's fold and then dwelling there safely, securely, and serenely for time and eternity.

The Lord Jesus Christ once told the 'Parable of the Lost Sheep' (see Luke 15:3–7). As the shepherd in this parable spared himself no pain in going after the lost sheep, Christ spared no pains to rescue us. He left heaven for earth to die on the cross of Calvary to save us. Jesus said: 'The Son of Man has come to seek and to save that which was lost' (Luke 19:10) and 'I am the Good Shepherd. The Good Shepherd gives His life for the sheep' (John 10:11).

Salvation, then, in the personal experience of the saved, is a returning to the safety of the flock of God. With both Isaiah's prophecy and the Saviour's parable in mind, Peter could write to his Christian readers 'For you were like sheep going astray, but have now returned to the Shepherd and Overseer of your souls' (1 Peter 2:25). Once we have been rescued and returned to God's fold, we are saved, safe and secure for all eternity! The Bible teaches the eternal security of the soul united to Christ. None of Christ's rescued and restored will ever perish. Jesus said, 'My sheep hear My voice, and I know them, and they follow Me; and I give them eternal life and they shall never perish, neither shall anyone snatch them out of My hand' (John 10:27, 28). Interestingly, the famous Psalm which begins by affirming 'The LORD is my shepherd' (Psalm 23:1) ends by declaring 'and I will dwell in the house of the LORD for ever' (Psalm 23:6).

Stray sheep, then, are pitiful creatures. Sin is a pitiful and damnable state. The gospel of Christ alone offers hope to stray sinners with imperilled souls. God in Christ has taken the initiative for our salvation. He is a God of supernatural, sovereign and saving grace. 'All we like sheep have gone astray; we have turned every one to his own way; and the LORD has laid on Him the iniquity of us all' (Isaiah 53:6).

Reflect on these points

1. *List some of the earthly and eternal consequences of (a) Human sin (b) Divine salvation.*
2. *Consider: 'A defective view of sin will lead to a defective view of salvation. A right view of sin will lead to a right view of salvation.'*
3. *Is it true to say that only a Christian can truly affirm 'The LORD is my shepherd.' (Psalm 23:1)?*

The silence

'He was oppressed, and He was afflicted, yet He opened not His mouth; He was led as a lamb to the slaughter, and as a sheep before its shearers is silent, so He opened not His mouth.'

Isaiah 53:7

Even those who were not Christ's followers were forced to admit that no one ever opened his mouth to speak like He did: 'No man ever spoke like this Man' (John 7:46). Three times in our title verse, though, Isaiah is impressed by the silence, rather than the speech, of the Suffering Servant who was to come. 'He opened not His mouth.'

The Silence of the Saviour

In the fullness of time, Isaiah's prophecy was certainly fulfilled in the Lord Jesus Christ. Matthew records how, at His trial before the Jewish authorities, 'Jesus kept silent' (Matthew 26:63) when He was both vilified and victimised by false witnesses. Then a little later, standing before Pontius Pilate the Roman governor, Matthew records that 'while He was being accused by the chief priests and elders, He answered nothing' (Matthew 27:12). Matthew continues 'Then Pilate said to Him, "Do you not hear how many things they testify against You?" And He answered him not one word, …' (Matthew 27:13, 14). In the same vein, Luke records that, before Jesus was condemned to death, King Herod 'questioned Him with many words, but He answered him nothing' (Luke 23:9).

A tender plant from the dry ground

This silence of the Saviour before His enemies and accusers is especially striking when we recall the power which was at His disposal to destroy them all in an instant. Jesus had said previously, 'Do you think that I cannot now pray to My Father, and He will provide Me with more than twelve legions (that is approximately 72,000) of angels?' (Matthew 26:53). Years later, perhaps with the above in mind, Peter wrote of his Friend and Saviour 'When He was reviled, did not revile in return; when He suffered, He did not threaten, but committed Himself to Him Who judges righteously' (1 Peter 2:23).

According to Ecclesiastes 3:7, there is 'a time to keep silence, and a time to speak.' How, then, are we to understand the silence of the Suffering Servant? The silence of the Suffering Servant prophesied by Isaiah may be understood in two ways: (a) The Silence of Sin and (b) The Silence of Submission.

(A) THE SILENCE OF SIN

We sometimes use the expression 'a guilty silence.' A guilty silence occurs when we are convicted of our sin, guilt and culpability. We have no excuse to make. We cannot make any pleadings or pleas as to our innocence. It is the law of God that shuts our mouths. God's law condemns the sinner to a damned doom. 'Now we know that whatever the law says it says to those under the law, so that every mouth may be stopped, and all the world may become guilty before God' (Romans 3:19).

How, then, is the Servant's silence explained? Because He was accounted guilty. Although sinless Himself, He bore the sin and guilt of others. The sinless One was accounted guilty

The silence

so that sinners may be accounted righteous and be eternally acquitted for His sake. 'For He made Him who knew no sin to be sin for us, that we might become the righteousness of God in Him' (2 Corinthians 5:21). We have seen that 'All we like sheep have gone astray …' (Isaiah 53:6). Here, then, is One who stood in the place of straying sheep, and bore their sin and judgment, 'He was led as a lamb to the slaughter and as a sheep before its shearers is silent, so He opened not His mouth' (Isaiah 53:7). Christ's silence, then, may be explained with reference to our guilty silence and His paying the penalty for our sins. The silence of Christ though may also be explained in terms of:

(b) The Silence of Submission

The Lord Jesus was sent into the world on a mission from His Father. He came into the world to accomplish the salvation of God's people. 'For God did not send His Son into the world to condemn the world, but that the world through Him might be saved' (John 3:17). Christ was obedient to His Father's will. Hence, when He was accused and condemned to death, He was silent. No force in the universe could ever make Him open His mouth and speak up in His own defence, so determined was He to accomplish His Father's will and fulfill His eternal plan of salvation.

Christ thus silently submitted to His Father's will '… He humbled Himself and became obedient to the point of death, even the death of the cross' (Philippians 2:8).

Theologians distinguish between Christ's active and

passive obedience—although the two are very much enmeshed and complementary. Christ's active obedience concerns His complete keeping of God's law and willingness to lay down His perfectly guiltless and sinless life as a sacrifice for sinners. He stated 'I lay down My life that I may take it again. No one takes it from Me, but I lay it down of Myself' (John 10:17, 18). His passive obedience though, writes Berkhof, 'consisted in His paying the penalty of our sin by His sufferings and death, and thus discharging the debt of all His people.'[1]

Christ was also silently submissive during the three dark hours when He endured the wrath of God on Calvary's cross:

> Silent through those three dread hours
> Wrestling with the evil powers
> Left alone with human sin
> Gloom around Thee and within
> Till the appointed time is nigh
> Till the Lamb of God may die.[2]

Christ's silent submission, though, wrought our salvation. Eventually He broke His silence with the triumphant acclamation and affirmation '"It is finished!" and bowing His head, He gave up His spirit' (John 19:30).

So thank God for the Saviour's speech, but thank God for the Saviour's silence, too. 'He was led as a lamb to the slaughter, and as a sheep that before its shearers is silent, so He opened not His mouth.'

The silence

Reflect on these points

1. 'No man ever spoke like this Man' (John 7:46). Sceptics say that Jesus never actually claimed to be God. Is this so? (Look up Mark 16:61, 62 and John 13:13).
2. What do we learn from the Saviour's silence in our chapter verse?
3. Is it possible to testify to Christ by our silence as well as by our speech?
4. We know that words can wound. This being so, pray over Psalm 141:3 and Proverbs 13:3.
5. Does God's will entail passive obedience as well as active obedience?

The sheep

'*He was led as a lamb to the slaughter, and as a sheep before its shearers is silent, so He opened not His mouth.*'

Isaiah 53:7

The Centrality of the Lamb

Isaiah's prophetic foresight enabled him to foresee the coming Suffering Servant of the Lord as being like 'a lamb that is led to the slaughter'. This is highly significant. Isaiah's prophecy here is nothing novel but altogether in line with the whole of the Bible, for the Lamb and its significance is one of the Bible's unifying themes:

If we wanted to summarise the message of the Old Testament, we could do so by using Isaac's question to his father Abraham: 'Where is the lamb?' (Genesis 22:7). Abraham's answer that 'God will provide for Himself the lamb' (Genesis 22:8) encapsulates Old Testament prophecy in general and Isaiah's fifty third chapter in particular.

If we wanted to summarise the message of the New Testament, we could do so by utilising John the Baptist's words in John 1:29: 'Behold! The Lamb of God, who takes away the sin of the world!' John was pointing to the Lord Jesus here. The unanimous witness of the New Testament is that He is *the Lamb of God*—a Lamb who was slaughtered so that sinners could be saved.

If we wanted to summarise the testimony of the Christian, both now and for all eternity, we could do so by employing the words of Revelation 5:12: 'Worthy is the Lamb who was slain.' For the Christian owes everything to Jesus, the Lamb of God who died to secure the eternal redemption of God's elect. 'He was led as a lamb to the slaughter, and as a sheep before its shearers is silent, so He opened not His mouth.'

The Passover Lamb

The Exodus from Egypt is a central event in Old Testament history, and central to this central event was the slaying of the Passover lamb. Exodus 12 gives the details:

The people of Israel were in cruel bondage in the land of Egypt. Pharaoh, the king of Egypt, was hardened against them and would not release them from their slavery. Almighty God, though, stepped in on behalf of His people and softened Pharaoh's heart so that he eventually relented and released the Israelites from their cruel incarceration. He sent a series of plagues on Egypt and Pharaoh. These, however, seemed to harden Pharaoh's heart further. They did so until the final plague. The final plague was death to every first-born in the land without discrimination.

To Moses and the Israelites, however, God revealed a way of escape from this death and judgment. Paradoxically, this also entailed a death—the death of a substitute. God ordained that if a spotless, unblemished lamb was taken and slain, and its blood applied to the house, the inhabitants of that house would come to no harm. 'The blood shall be a sign for you on the houses where you are. And when I see the blood, I will pass over you; and the plague shall not be on you to destroy you when I strike the land of Egypt' (Exodus 12:13).

The sheep

The Israelites alone were privy to these instructions concerning the Passover lamb, and they duly obeyed the divine injunctions to the letter: They selected a spotless lamb, killed it, applied its blood and waited ... And it all happened just as God had said it would. There was sorrow and death in the Egyptian homes, but salvation and rejoicing in the Israelites'. The angel of death 'passed over' them. They were sheltering under the Passover blood. Because the lamb had been killed, they escaped the judgment of death that was the lot of the Egyptians. Pharaoh was horrified and his heart melted. He screamed out 'Be gone' (Exodus 12:32) to the Israelites, and the children of Abraham were released from their bondage. The slain lamb had redeemed them, that is, it had set them free.

The Passover Lamb

The Passover lamb—a lamb which brought deliverance from death and judgment in Moses' day—is one of the clearest types of Christ in the Old Testament. If we are sheltering under Christ's blood to save us, we are safe from eternal death and judgment. Christ died in our place to save us from death and judgment. If we belong to Jesus, God sees us 'in Christ'—saved by virtue of what He has done. Considering that the work of Christ at Calvary has so many parallels with the work which the Passover lamb effected at the time of the Exodus, the New Testament often views Calvary in Passover terms. Christ is the Passover Lamb, and His death has wrought an even greater redemption:

'For indeed Christ, our Passover, was sacrificed for us' (1 Corinthians 5:7).

'In Him we have redemption through His blood …' (Ephesians 1:7).

'… redeemed … with the precious blood of Christ, as of a lamb without blemish and without spot' (1 Peter 1:18, 19).

Worthy is the Lamb
So Christ is the sinless, Passover Lamb. He died at Calvary to save us from eternal death and judgment. He shed His precious blood to effect our deliverance. The lamb, then, is integral to the divine revelation. Hence Isaiah spoke of the coming Redeemer in these terms too: 'He was led as a lamb to the slaughter, and as a sheep before its shearers is silent, so He opened not His mouth' (Isaiah 53:7).

Isaiah's message therefore—the message of the substitutionary Saviour—is one with the New Testament. In Isaiah, it is a case of history interpreting prophecy and, unusually, prophecy interpreting history. Isaiah was mouthing the same words as John the Baptist. Pointing us to Christ, he says 'Behold! The Lamb of God …' (John 1:29). Isaiah foresaw not just the Lamb but the Lamb who was slain.

The sheep

Reflect on these points

1. *How would you explain Christ's being 'the Lamb of God' (John 1:29) to one who is a stranger to the worldview of the Bible?*
2. *Heaven's praise goes 'Worthy is the Lamb who was slain' (Revelation 5:12). Ponder these words and take time to enter into the spirit of heaven's worship.*
3. *'The Lamb and its significance is one of the Bible's unifying themes.' Using a concordance, show that this is so.*

The stricken

'He was taken from prison and from judgment, and who will declare His generation? For He was cut off from the land of the living; for the transgression of My people He was stricken.'

Isaiah 53:8

The Stricken Servant

In our verse here, Isaiah foresaw that the coming Suffering Servant was to suffer a cruel, violent and, humanly speaking, premature death. He was to be 'cut off from the land of the living'. A prophecy made by the prophet Daniel some years later tallies exactly with this prophecy of Isaiah. Daniel, too, prophesied that 'Messiah shall be cut off, but not for Himself' (Daniel 9:26).

That the Lord Jesus Christ is the only fulfillment of both Isaiah's and Daniel's prophecies is the clear testimony of the New Testament. The New Testament emphasis is far more on the death of Christ than on His life. The Saviour Himself also spoke of His ministry as being primarily concerned with His dying, as opposed to His living—this in spite of the fact that no one ever lived like the Lord Jesus Christ, and no one life ever accomplished more than His. Christ, however, always lived with His impending death in mind. He lived under the shadow of His coming cross, hence He could prophesy of Himself: 'The Son of Man is being delivered into the hands of men, and they will kill Him. And after He is killed, He will rise the third day' (Mark 9:31).

To understand the Bible's emphasis on the death of Christ,

we have to understand the nature of death itself, according to the Bible.

Death: Physical, Spiritual and Eternal

According to the Bible, death is God's judgment on sin. Sin originated in Eden with our first ancestors. God warned them that they would die if they disobeyed His commandment not to eat of the fruit of the tree of the knowledge of good and evil. 'Of the fruit of the tree which is in the midst of the garden, God has said, "You shall not eat of it, nor shall you touch it, lest you *die*"' (Genesis 3:3). What ensued is well known. Adam and Eve disobeyed God and so brought His judgment down on themselves. Straightaway they died spiritually, for their harmonious relationship with their Maker was now destroyed. Eventually, they also died physically, for God pronounced, 'Dust you are, and to dust you shall return' (Genesis 3:19). It is human sin, then, that is responsible for the sad fact of death. Scripture unanimously links sin and death throughout its pages, as cause and effect. Death is a consequence of sin:

> 'The soul who sins shall die' (Ezekiel 18:4).

> 'Therefore, just as through one man sin entered the world, and death through sin, and thus death spread to all men because all sinned' (Romans 5:12).

> 'The wages of sin is death' (Romans 6:23).

'Death', though, according to the Bible, has various facets

The stricken

to it. There is physical death (compare 'Joseph died ... and he was put in a coffin in Egypt'—see Genesis 50:26) which refers to the separation of the soul from the body. But the Bible also teaches that there is spiritual death as well. Spiritual death refers to the separation of the soul from God. Sin separates us from God, and thus makes us spiritually dead even when we are physically alive. This will remain the case unless God intervenes in His mercy and regenerating grace. Ephesians 2:1 is clear: 'And you He made alive, who were *dead* in trespasses and sins in which you once walked ...'

Spiritual death, upon physical death, leads to the greatest terror of all which is eternal death. Eternal death refers to the eternal separation of the soul from God—eternal separation from God's love, light and life. Eternal death is referred to in various ways in the Bible. Synonyms include such words as hell, God's wrath, God's curse, perdition, the lake of fire and 'the second death'.

So the Bible teaches that death—the king of terrors and 'the last enemy'—has three dreadful facets to it. Death is physical, spiritual and eternal. It is necessary to know this as it is the necessary backcloth to the gospel. The bad news precedes the good. The diagnosis precedes the cure. The gospel is that Jesus died to save us from death in all of its terrible facets. Hence Isaiah, the 'evangelical prophet' foretold of Christ's suffering 'prison and ... judgment' and being 'cut off from the land of the living; for the transgression of My people He was stricken.'

A tender plant from the dry ground

The Death of Christ

On the cross of Calvary, the Christ foretold by Isaiah died both physically and spiritually. The death of the eternal Son of God in time was a death of eternal moment. The gospel proclaims that 'Christ died for our sins' (1 Corinthians 15:3) and 'Christ died for the ungodly' (Romans 5:6). Death is God's judgment on sin, and when Christ died, He suffered God's judgment on sin. He suffered so, not for His own sins, for He had none. He suffered and died for the sins of others. 'For the transgression of My people He was stricken.' Isaiah, then, is repeating and reiterating a theme which runs throughout his famous prophecy, namely that the sinless One was to die in the place of sinners, as their substitute, to save them from the dreadful, deathly, damnable plight which is their just due because of their sin. He was punished so sinners could be pardoned. His death, paradoxically, saves from death. Believers in Christ 'shall not be hurt by the second death' (Revelation 2:11).

Life by His Death

The Saviour then, paradoxically, died to give us life—that eternal life which is unblemished fellowship with God. His death on the cross for our sins takes the sting of death away. 'The wages of sin is death but the gift of God is eternal life in Christ Jesus our Lord' (Romans 6:23). He endured God's wrath in our place—'He Himself is the propitiation for our sins' (1 John 2:2). His death for our sins reconciles us to God for time and eternity.

In a truly dreadful moment, Christ, on the cross, was separated from His Father. He experienced spiritual death. Our sin, when laid upon Him, made Him suffer hell itself, so that He cried, 'My God, my God, why have You forsaken Me?' (Matthew 27:46). The darkness and dereliction of Calvary truly was the most dreadful moment in history. Yet, paradoxically, it was also the most wonderful, for Christ's hell wrought the believer's right to heaven, and Christ's separation wrought the believer's eternal reconciliation. 'Christ also suffered once for sins, the just for the unjust, that He might bring us to God' (1 Peter 3:18). The Christian gospel is a gospel of reconciliation. Sinners may be reconciled to God by the atoning death of Christ. As Christians we 'rejoice in God through our Lord Jesus Christ, through whom we have now received the reconciliation' (Romans 5:11).

The Death of Christ and the Evangelistic Task

Hence we see the centrality, necessity and meaning of Christ's unique death in both Isaiah's prophecy and in the whole of the Bible. His death was for our sins. It is by believing in the crucified Christ that we partake of the benefits of His death and receive God's salvation. Christ's death gives us new life! Believers will never experience the second death. Conversely, non-believers—those who have been born once physically, but have never been born again spiritually—will die twice. Non-Christians will die both physically and eternally—eternally separated from the love of God and the God of love.

It is the nature of both death and the death of Christ which makes the preaching of the gospel such an urgent task. The Church's mission and commission is to get sinners to the foot of the cross. 'We preach Christ crucified' (1 Corinthians 1:23). 'For the message of the cross is foolishness to those who are perishing, but to us who are being saved it is the power of God' (1 Corinthians 1:18). The nearness of eternity and the certainty of God's judgment makes the evangelistic task absolutely imperative. All preachers of the gospel know something of the apostolic imperative as they go about their life-calling, and urge sinners separated from God to trust the crucified, reconciling Saviour. 'We are ambassadors for Christ, as though God were pleading through us: we implore you on Christ's behalf, be reconciled to God' (2 Corinthians 5:20).

Isaiah's famous prophecy, then, was a 'cruciform' prophecy. He foresaw the Christ of Calvary. He saw Christ's sufferings. His sufferings were the worst imaginable, and yet they were purposeful and not pointless. On the cross 'He was cut off from the land of the living; for the transgression of My people He was stricken.' This is, and will always be, the joy of God's redeemed.

Reflect on these points

1. *Seemingly, 'Anything goes' today, yet death is still a taboo subject. Why do you think that this is so?*
2. *What does the Bible mean when it refers to 'death'?*
3. *Why should death—'the last enemy' (1 Corinthians 15:26)—hold no fear for the Christian? What is the basis of Christian assurance?*

The Scriptures

'And they made His grave with the wicked—but with the rich at His death ...'

Isaiah 53:9

The detailed fulfillment of this prophecy in Christ, some seven hundred years after it was first uttered by Isaiah, is one of the many evidences that the Bible is the Word of God. The eternal God alone knows the future, and hence the eternal God alone can reveal the future, if He so wishes. In Isaiah 44:7 God issues the following challenge to idols: 'Who can proclaim as I do? Then let him declare it and set it in order for Me ... And the things that are coming and shall come, let them show these to them.' Similarly, in Isaiah 46:10 He describes Himself as the One 'declaring the end from the beginning and from ancient times things that are not yet done' and then asserts 'I have spoken it; I will bring it to pass; I have purposed it; I will also do it' (Isaiah 46:11).

The fulfillment of prophecy is also, according to the law of Moses, the touchstone as to whether the prophet in question was speaking from God or merely projecting thoughts woven from his own imagination. There was a distinct criterion to consider when someone uttered a predictive prophecy. Deuteronomy 18:21, 22 stated 'And if you say in your heart, "How shall we know the word which the Lord has not spoken?"—when a prophet speaks in the name of the Lord, if the thing does not happen or come to pass, that is the thing which the Lord has

A tender plant from the dry ground

not spoken; the prophet has spoken it presumptuously; you shall not be afraid of him.'

Isaiah 53:9 was fulfilled to the letter in the Lord Jesus Christ, in the fullness of time. The exact and precise fulfillment of the prophecy is inexplicable apart from the divine inspiration of the Scriptures—that Isaiah was one of the 'holy men of God' who 'spoke as they were moved by the Holy Spirit'(2 Peter 1:21). Christ's grave was indeed both 'with the wicked' and 'with the rich at His death.'

(A) 'THEY MADE HIS GRAVE WITH THE WICKED ...'
Seven hundred years after Isaiah spoke this particular prophecy, the Lord Jesus Christ was crucified along with two criminals. Luke records how 'There were also two others, criminals, led with Him to be put to death' (Luke 23:32). Matthew is a little more explicit about the nature of the wickedness of the two who were put to death with Christ. He states, 'Then two robbers were crucified with Him, one on the right and another on the left' (Matthew 27:38).

Christ was thus treated with the 'lowest of the low'. His innocence notwithstanding, He received the same treatment as two thieves—thieves who had been tried and considered worthy of the ultimate punishment meted out by a human court: capital punishment. As an aside, we notice that Luke's account records the salvation of one of these nameless thieves. One, while dying, turned to the Lord Jesus. He confessed Christ's crimelessness, and asked to be remembered by Him. Jesus said to him, 'Assuredly, I say to you, today you will be

The Scriptures

with Me in Paradise' (Luke 23:43). Here is a trophy of grace! The dying thief was a saved sinner. Every Christian who has ever lived would testify to being the same.

So Christ's death was an ignominious death. He was crucified with two criminals. 'They made His grave with the wicked.' It would seem also that His burial would be no different from their burial. Criminals were not given any dignified burial, but rather just cast into a common grave. This befitted the contempt in which they were held. Almighty God though had His Word to fulfill in the case of His Suffering Servant:

(B) 'THEY MADE HIS GRAVE ... WITH THE RICH AT HIS DEATH ...'

Against the odds, this Scripture was also fulfilled down to its smallest detail. Christ was given a special, careful, loving and dignified burial. It is here that a certain rich man comes on to the centre stage. The rich man in question was one Joseph of Arimathea. Matthew records the events of the evening of the first 'Good Friday' so:

'Now when was evening, there came a rich man from Arimathea, named Joseph, who himself had also become a disciple of Jesus. This man went to Pilate and asked for the body of Jesus. Then Pilate commanded the body to be given to him. And when Joseph had taken the body, he wrapped it in a clean linen cloth, and laid it in his new tomb which he had hewn out of the rock; and he rolled a large stone against the door of the tomb, and departed' (Matthew 27:57 f.). As the Lord Jesus Himself said shortly before His death: 'For I say

A tender plant from the dry ground

to you that this which is written must still be accomplished in Me' (Luke 22:37).

So the Christ who inhabited a virgin womb also inhabited a virgin tomb. Under God, Joseph of Arimathea saw to it. Joseph of Arimathea was a rich man, and had means at his disposal—means which were utilised by Almighty God to fulfill His Word. And it was out of this rich man's tomb that the crucified Christ arose! 'He was buried … He rose again the third day according to the Scriptures' (1 Corinthians 15:4). The resurrection of Christ has been termed 'the most attested fact in history', and on this attested fact the truth of the Christian faith is founded. The Christ who died for and alongside sinners—'the wicked'—and was buried in a rich man's tomb also conquered the grave on the third day. He was 'declared to be the Son of God with power, according to the Spirit of holiness, by the resurrection from the dead …' (Romans 1:4).

The Scriptures

Reflect on these points

1. *'Fulfilled prophecy is one evidence that the Bible is the Word of God.' List some other Old Testament prophecies which were all fulfilled in Christ.*
2. *'All Scripture is given by inspiration of God …' (2 Timothy 3:16). Why is belief in the divine inspiration of Scripture so foundational to the Christian faith?*
3. *What evidence other than fulfilled prophecy may be adduced to prove that the Bible is no ordinary book but 'the Word of God written'?*

The sinlessness

'... He had done no violence, nor was any deceit in His mouth.'

Isaiah 53:9

Isaiah is here asserting the Servant's total innocence. He did not deserve to be put to death, he says, because He was innocent and crimeless. He had done no wrong at all—'He had done no violence, nor was any deceit in His mouth.'

Isaiah's assertion is an important one, for only a sinless One could save sinners. If the Servant was not sinless, He would be dying for His own sins and not for the sins of others. This would make a complete mockery of Isaiah's central thesis that the Servant was dying as our substitute—'wounded for *our* transgressions ... bruised for *our* iniquities' (Isaiah 53:5, emphasis mine).

The high priest, from Aaron onwards, was 'required as for the people, so also for himself, to offer sacrifices for sins' (Hebrews 5:3). The coming Servant prophesied by Isaiah however was to be very different. As this Servant was sinless in His being, the punishment He was to endure was not because of His owns sins, but for the sins of others. We state again, then, that only a sinless One is capable and qualified to be the Saviour of sinners. Just as at the time of the Exodus, the Passover lamb—the lamb which was sacrificed—had to be 'without blemish' (Exodus 12:5) and 'perfect' (Leviticus 22:21) or else it would be of no saving avail, so the Saviour, too, had to be morally 'without blemish' and 'perfect' if His life given up in sacrifice was to be of a saving benefit to sinners.

The Sinless Saviour

The unanimous testimony of the New Testament is that Christ was sinless. Uniquely of those born of women, Christ was impeccable, that is, He was completely untainted by sin. He was sinless in His very nature, and hence sinless in practice—He never thought, spoke or did anything contrary to the will of God. Let us call in the witnesses to this:

Paul stated that Christ 'knew no sin' (2 Corinthians 5:21). Hebrews 7:26 describes Him as being 'holy, harmless, undefiled, separate from sinners'. One of the thieves put to death with Jesus, while admitting the justice of his own sentence, confessed of Christ that 'this Man has done nothing wrong' (Luke 23:41). Pilate—the one, humanly speaking, who had the power to pronounce whether Christ was crucified or not—gave his verdict on Christ, so: 'What evil has He done? I have found no reason for death in Him' (Luke 23:22). The apostle Peter said the Christ 'committed no sin' (1 Peter 2:22), and the apostle John said that 'in Him there is no sin' (1 John 3:5). These last two testimonies are remarkable in that Peter and John were part of the inner circle of three of the twelve disciples. They were especially close to Jesus during the years of His earthly ministry. Normally, the closer we get to people, the more aware we become of their faults, failings and flaws. Character blemishes otherwise hidden from a public role and persona come into sharper focus when we get to know someone more intimately and privately. This was not the case with the Lord Jesus Christ though.

The sinlessness of Jesus Christ has never been challenged throughout the years of history. It was never even challenged during His time on earth. Jesus alone of the human race could say truthfully, 'I always do those things that please Him [God the Father]' (John 8:29) and throw down a gauntlet to His antagonists and ask, 'Which of you convicts Me of sin?' (John 8:46).

The Scriptures therefore teach that in Christ we have a sinless Saviour. His sinlessness is one of the qualifications which qualifies Him for being the Saviour. He died, not for His own sins, but for the sins of others. He was 'delivered up for our offences' (Romans 4:25) and 'wounded for our transgressions ... for the transgressions of My people He was stricken' (Isaiah 53:5, 8).

Returning to our title text from Isaiah 53, we note that Isaiah states that the Servant's sinlessness lies in both His conduct and His conversation—His walk and His words: 'He had done no violence, nor was any deceit in His mouth' (Isaiah 53:9). It is highly likely that the apostle Peter had this specific prophecy in mind when, reminiscing about Christ's life on earth, he wrote of Him: 'Who committed no sin, nor was guile found in His mouth, who, when He was reviled, did not revile in return; when He suffered, He did not threaten; but committed Himself to Him Who judges righteously' (1 Peter 2:22, 23).

Specifically then, Isaiah speaks of:

A tender plant from the dry ground

(A) The Saviour's Sinless Conduct

'He had done no violence …' 1 John 3:4 states that 'Sin is lawlessness.' Violence has no rules and is an example of lawlessness. Violence refers to the unlawful exercise of physical force. One of the reasons given for God's judgment of the ancient world by a universal flood was because 'the earth was filled with violence' (Genesis 6:11). Christ was the complete antithesis of violence. He said, 'I am gentle and lowly in heart' (Matthew 11:29). Isaiah had previously written of Him that 'a bruised reed He will not break, and smoking flax He will not quench' (Isaiah 42:3).

Christ was certainly a victim of violence, but when cruel men hammered nails into His flesh and nailed Him to the cross, His response was to pray, 'Father, forgive them; for they do not know what they do' (Luke 23:34). In 2 Corinthians 10:1 Paul made mention of 'the meekness and gentleness of Christ.' Truly, He had done no violence, in thought, word or deed. Isaiah also however refers to:

(B) The Saviour's Sinless Conversation

'… nor was any deceit in His mouth.' To our shame, we sometimes deceive and lie in an attempt to cover up our sin. Telling lies is a result of human cowardice, convention, ignorance, weakness or depravity. But no lie ever crossed the Saviour's lips. His was a sinless speech.

Our habitual speech betrays the sort of people we are. Our speech is a reflection of our innermost hearts. Jesus said, 'What comes out of a man, that defiles him' (Mark 7:20). Elsewhere,

The sinlessness

Jesus said that speaking 'bad' words is a consequence of possessing a corrupt heart. Hence our need for regeneration: 'For a good tree does not bear bad fruit, nor does a bad tree bear good fruit … A good man out of the good treasure of his heart brings forth good; and an evil man out of the evil treasure of his heart brings forth evil. For out of the abundance of the heart his mouth speaks' (Luke 6:43–45).

The external conversation which Christ spoke then reflected the innermost character of who He was. He alone was a true 'good man'. He was sinless in His being. His cruel killing as a common criminal was totally unjust, for 'He had done no violence, nor was any deceit in His mouth.' There is an infinite, qualitative difference between the Saviour and those whom He came to save. Christ was 'without sin' (Hebrews 4:15). Hence He was able to offer up His life as a perfect sacrifice on behalf of sinners.

> Guilty, vile and helpless we
> Spotless Lamb of God was He
> Full atonement!—can it be?
> Hallelujah! What a Saviour![1]

A tender plant from the dry ground

Reflect on these points

1. *Why is it so essential to hold to Christ's impeccability? List some of the Scriptural evidence which proves Christ's absolute sinlessness.*
2. *Christ's sinless nature was revealed by both His conduct and His conversation. If you were on trail for being a Christian, would your conduct and conversation be such to convict you that you have been truly born again?*
3. *Jesus said, 'Out of the abundance of the heart [the] mouth speaks' (Luke 6:45). Is the language we habitually use the cause or the consequence of our spiritual condition?*

The surprise

The sovereignty

'Yet it pleased the Lord to bruise Him; He has put Him to grief ...'

Isaiah 53:10

Isaiah is here stating that the ultimate cause of the Servant's terrible suffering was not the will of man but the will of God. It was Almighty God who ordained and ensured that His Servant should suffer as He did. Heaven had its method and reason, and this method and reason was worked out on earth in due time. The will of the Lord was fulfilled when His own Son came and 'was killed by hanging on a tree' (Acts 10:39). Divine sovereignty and human responsibility coalesced at Calvary. In fact, the divine will was worked out through the will of cruel men. As Paul proclaimed in the synagogue in Pisidian Antioch: 'those who dwell in Jerusalem, and their rulers, because they did not know Him, nor even the voices of the prophets which are read every Sabbath, have fulfilled them in condemning Him. And though they found no cause for death in Him, they asked Pilate that He should be put to death' (Acts 13:27, 28).

The relationship between divine sovereignty and human responsibility is, of course, beyond our human comprehension. Scripture teaches both, and we will do well to hold them both in tension. The Bible teaches that the ultimate cause of Christ's death was the will of God. Yet the Bible also teaches that those who were humanly responsible for Christ's death were free and rational agents in all that they did, and thus fully culpable.

Who killed Christ?

The answer to the question 'Who was responsible for the death of Christ?' is a complex one:

(a) It was Judas Iscariot, one of the twelve chosen disciples, who betrayed Jesus, handing Him over to the Jewish authorities.

(b) It was the Jewish authorities who were then adamant that 'He is deserving of death' (Matthew 26:66), for they considered Jesus' claim to be the Son of God blasphemous.

(c) It was the Roman governor, Pontius Pilate, who eventually succumbed to pressure and authorised the death of Christ. He gave in to crowd pressure and literally washed his hands of the proceedings: 'The Jews said to him "It is not lawful for us to put anyone to death."' (John 18:31). Luke records that 'the chief priests, the rulers and the people … were insistent, demanding with loud voices that He be crucified. And the voices of these men and the chief priests prevailed. So Pilate gave sentence that it should be as they requested … He delivered Jesus to their will' (Luke 23:13, 23 f.).

(d) It was some nameless, Roman soldiers, supervised by a Roman centurion, who were responsible for the grizzly task of actually hammering the nails into the flesh of the Son of God. 'And when they had come to the place called Calvary, there they crucified Him …' (Luke 23:33).

All the above are true. Yet underlying the will of men with their cruel intentions and mixed motives, lay the sovereign will of God. 'It pleased the LORD to bruise Him; He has put Him to grief.' In the crucified Christ the eternal will of God to save His people was worked out in time. As Peter explained in his sermon on the Day of Pentecost: 'Him, [the Lord Jesus], being delivered by the determined counsel and foreknowledge of God, you have taken by lawless hands, have crucified, and put to death' (Acts 2:23).

Looking behind all 'secondary causes', therefore, the ultimate explanation of the death of Christ is the will of God. Even this most cruel and wicked of human acts was divinely ordained—ordained for the salvation of souls and the glory of God.

The Divine Decrees

According to the Bible, nothing ever occurs by accident or chance. Rather, all that has happened and all that ever will happen is due to the will of God. He is almighty, omnipotent, sovereign and supreme. The Shorter Catechism states:

'The decrees of God are His eternal purpose, according to the counsel of His will, whereby, for His Own glory, He hath foreordained whatsoever comes to pass.'[1]

The Bible states that: 'For of Him and through Him and to Him are *all* things' (Romans 11:36, emphasis mine). He 'works *all things* according to the counsel of His will' (Ephesians 1:11, emphasis mine).

God's redemption of His people, then, may be considered as the outworking of His eternal providence. Integral to God's providential plan of redemption is the death of His Son at Calvary. God sent His Son to procure the salvation of those whom He eternally chose—and God sends His Spirit to apply this work of redemption to those same people. Hence the death of Christ at Calvary was no dire accident but a divine appointment. Almighty God ensured that His Son would pay the wages of sin in full. 'It pleased the LORD to bruise Him; He has put Him to grief.' In the Christ of Calvary, Almighty God was bringing His eternal plan into effect. Looking behind the human actors and actions, then, we state that the root explanation of Calvary was the sovereign grace of God to His people: 'He ... did not spare His own Son but delivered Him up for us all' (Romans 8:32). 'In this is love, not that we loved God but that He loved us and sent His Son to be the propitiation for our sins' (1 John 4:10).

The cruel and ignominious death of Christ at Calvary, as prophesied in Isaiah 53, is, paradoxically, the supreme demonstration of the sin of man and the love, justice and sovereignty of God. When the sin and inhumanity of man is rampant, the Christian, with Calvary in mind, can yet affirm 'Alleluia! For the Lord God omnipotent reigns' (Revelation 19:6).

Reflect on these points

1. *What is the real answer to the question, 'Who killed Jesus?'*
2. *Consider this statement: 'Our only absolute comfort is the absolute sovereignty of God.'*
3. *Think of some other examples in the Bible when the perfect will of God was accomplished through the imperfect will of human beings.*
4. *'Those who see the hand of God in everything can leave everything in the hand of God.' Think of this statement in relation to your own life, especially as regards the darker providences you have experienced. Memorise Romans 8:28.*

The sacrifice

'When You make His soul an offering for sin ...'

Isaiah 53:10

Animal sacrifice, or 'offerings', were part of the very warp and woof of the Old Testament economy. The sacrificial system was not a human institution but instituted by God Himself. It was His gracious provision to deal with the human 'sin problem'—to deal with the sin and guilt which bars and mars the fellowship with our Maker which is our chief end.

In this verse, Isaiah prophesies that the coming Servant would Himself be 'an offering for sin'. Literally, He would be 'a guilt offering'. By the giving up of Himself in the place of sinners, He would deal with the guilt of their sin. The technical term for this is 'expiation'. To expiate means to remove guilt, making amends for it by paying its penalty. Again, Isaiah was spanning the centuries to the cross of Christ.

The Servant's Self-giving

Notice that Isaiah stresses the Servant's self-giving. 'When You make His soul an offering for sin ...' According to Isaiah, the Servant's life was not so much taken from Him by wicked men, but rather given up by Him voluntarily on behalf of the wicked. '... He poured out His soul unto death ...' (Isaiah 53:12). Here again, Isaiah's prophecy has only one fulfilment. It was fulfilled in the events of Good Friday, outside the walls of Jerusalem in the death of Christ, when 'Christ ... through the eternal Spirit offered Himself without spot to God' (Hebrews 9:14).

The New Testament is unanimous when it records that

A tender plant from the dry ground

Christ's life was given up by Him in death, rather than taken from Him by others:

Jesus Himself explained in Mark 10:45 that 'The Son of Man came … to give His life a ransom for many.' Similarly, in John 10:17, 18 He further stressed: 'I lay down My life, that I may take it again. No one takes it from Me, but I lay it down of Myself. I have power to lay it down, and I have power to take it again …' These words are confirmed and corroborated by the actual facts of Calvary: Matthew, for instance, records how 'Jesus when He had cried out again with a loud voice, yielded up His spirit' (Matthew 27:50).

Then in the New Testament epistles, Paul states, 'Christ also has loved us and given Himself for us, an offering and a sacrifice to God for a sweet-smelling aroma' (Ephesians 5:2), and 'Christ also loved the church and gave Himself up for it …' (Ephesians 5:25). And the personal testimony of every Christian who has ever lived is that: 'the Son of God … loved me and gave Himself for me' (Galatians 2:20).

Hence Isaiah's prophecy came true. Christ's soul was indeed made 'an offering for sin'.

The Sacrificial System

The death of Christ in the New Testament cannot really be understood apart from reference to the sacrifices and offerings instituted by God in the Old Testament. Christ's death was a sacrifice—'an offering for sin …'

Leviticus 1–7 details for us 'The Law of the Offerings.' From this we see that there were five offerings and sacrifices

The sacrifice

instituted by God in Old Testament times. Leviticus 7:37, 38 provides a précis of these:

'This is the law of the burnt offering, the grain offering, the sin offering, the trespass offering … and the sacrifice of the peace offerings, which the LORD commanded Moses on Mount Sinai, on the day when He commanded the people of Israel to offer their offerings to the LORD …'

What, though, was the meaning and thinking behind the sacrifices and offerings of the Old Testament era? This is answered well in these words:

> Sacrifice is always made to God Himself. So only the best is good enough … Sacrifice is a way of approach to God … Sacrifice is a substitution … The death of the sacrificed animal was seen as taking the place of the person who brought the sacrifice. [1]

In other words, the sacrifices and offerings of the Old Testament were to atone for sin. Leviticus 17:11 encapsulates it all when it says, 'The life of the flesh is in the blood, and I have given it for you upon the altar to make atonement for your souls; for it is the blood that makes atonement for the soul.'

Yet questions could be asked about the efficacy and permanence of these sacrifices … The fact that they were offered continually, suggested that they could not atone for sin once and for all. Hebrews 10:1f. articulates this doubt when it says that 'the law [of Moses] … can never, with these same sacrifices which they offer continually year by year, make those

A tender plant from the dry ground

who approach perfect. For then would they not have ceased to be offered? For the worshippers, once purged, would have had no more consciousness of sins. But in those sacrifices there is a reminder of sins every year. For it is not possible that the blood of bulls and goats could take away sins.'

> Not all the blood of beasts
> On Jewish altars slain
> Could give the guilty conscience peace
> And take away the stain.
>
> But Christ the heavenly Lamb
> Takes all our guilt away
> A sacrifice of nobler name
> And richer blood than they. [2]

Christ is the answer

Isaiah, then, in our verse, was looking forward to a sacrifice which would end all sacrifices and put away sin permanently. 'When You make His soul an offering for sin.' The New Testament proclaims that when Christ gave Himself as a sacrifice on the 'altar' of Calvary's cross, He 'made there, by His one oblation of Himself once offered, a full, perfect and sufficient sacrifice, oblation and satisfaction for the sins of the whole world'.[3] Here, then, is a Sacrifice which renders all other sacrifices obsolete. Here is an offering which makes all earthly priests redundant. The sacrificial priesthood has been rendered for ever redundant since Christ offered Himself as an

The sacrifice

eternal sacrifice for sin, efficient and sufficient to save eternally those who put their faith in Him:

'This Man, after He had offered one sacrifice for sins forever, sat down at the right hand of God' (Hebrews 10:12).

'For by one single offering He has perfected forever those who are being sanctified' (Hebrews 10:14).

Isaiah, then, in directing us to the only true and perfect 'offering for sin', is taking us again to the heart of the Christian gospel. Isaiah is pointing us to the one sacrifice of Christ at Calvary—to that which Protestants refer to as 'the finished work of Christ'. Isaiah, the 'Evangelical Prophet', was proclaiming the eternal sacrifice of Calvary which alone can eternally save.

Reflect on these points

1. *Why is the death of Christ in the New Testament incomprehensible without some knowledge of the Old Testament?*
2. *Why is sacrifice so central in the Bible? If Almighty God is omnipotent, why can't He forgive sins without it?*
3. *List some Scriptures which prove that Christ's life was given by Him and not taken from Him.*
4. *Why is it true to say that the office of a human priest is now obsolete?*

The success

'When you make His soul an offering for sin, He shall see His seed, He shall prolong His days, and the pleasure of the LORD shall prosper in His hand.'

Isaiah 53:10

Remarkably, Isaiah is teaching us here that the cruel treatment that the Servant was to receive, along with the brutal taking away of His life by cruel hands, was a success, not a failure. Humanly speaking, what could be more tragic than a premature death? Christ was about thirty three years of age when He died, so, humanly speaking, He was cut off in His prime. But Isaiah is saying here that the Servant's death was a triumph, not a tragedy, and that Christ was a victor not a victim. The death of the Servant, prophesied Isaiah, would actually accomplish something marvellous—something marvellous which just would not have been accomplished had He not suffered and died in the way that He did.

Yet again, Isaiah's Old Testament prophecy is somewhat inexplicable were it not for our New Testament hindsight and its fulfillment in Christ. Peter wrote of 'The prophets ... who prophesied ... the sufferings of Christ and glories that would follow' (1 Peter 1:10, 11), and in our title verse, Isaiah the prophet is moving on from the sufferings of Christ to their glorious aftermath—to what His sufferings achieved. The sufferings of Christ were purposeful, not pointless. The will of the Lord prospered in His hand. Theologians distinguish between Christ's two states, namely (a) His state of humiliation and (b) His state of exaltation. We have, on the whole, been occupied with the former up until now. In this verse, though, Isaiah turns to the Saviour's subsequent state of exaltation. Specifically, Isaiah delineates Christ's (a) Progeny (b) Prolongation and (c) Prosperity.

(a) Christ's Progeny

'… He shall see His seed …' Christ's sacrifice, says Isaiah, will result in His begetting a spiritual offspring. Those spiritually dead because of their sins will receive new life because of Christ's work. Jesus taught the same: 'So must the Son of Man be lifted up, that whoever believes in Him should not perish but have eternal life' (John 3:14,15). When a person experiences the new birth, here is a clear indication of New Testament salvation. 'But as many as received Him, to them He gave the right to become children of God, even to those who believe in His Name: who were born, not of blood nor of the will of the flesh nor of the will of man, but of God'(John 1:12, 13). Similarly, the apostle Paul wrote of 'the washing of regeneration and renewing of the Holy Spirit, Whom He poured out on us abundantly through Jesus Christ our Saviour' (Titus 3:5, 6).

By nature, we are the children of wrath. By God's grace, and through trusting the crucified Saviour, we become the children of God. Adoption, along with regeneration—or rather the adoption resulting from regeneration—is another way in which the Bible would have us understand the multifaceted salvation which ensues from the work of Christ. 'God sent forth His Son ... so that we might receive the adoption as sons' (Galatians 4:4). That God, for Christ's sake, should ever adopt sinners into His family, for time and eternity, is and will for ever be a matter of heartfelt praise for the recipients of this blessing. 'Behold what manner of love the Father has bestowed on us, that we should be called children of God!' (1 John 3:1).

(b) Christ's Prolongation

'He shall prolong His days ...' Isaiah is telling us here that the death of the Servant would not actually be the end of the Servant. He would actually live on again after His death. Hence Isaiah can only be speaking of the resurrection of Christ. 'Whom they killed by hanging on a tree; Him God raised up on the third day and showed Him openly' (Acts 10:39, 40).

The resurrection of Christ has been well termed as 'the most attested fact of history'. The resurrection of Christ lies at the centre of the Christian faith. The earliest creedal summary of the basic fundamentals of the Christian faith states 'that Christ died for our sins in according to the Scriptures, and that He was buried, and that He rose again the third day according to the Scriptures'(1 Corinthians 15:3, 4). While in Athens, the apostle Paul 'preached to them Jesus and the resurrection' (Acts 17:18).

Christ's life was thus prolonged by God. God's raising of His Son from the grave on the first 'Easter Sunday' is the lynchpin in the evidence of the divine acceptance, good pleasure and satisfaction with Christ's atoning work on 'Good Friday'. God raised His Son from the grave! For the next forty days, Christ appeared to various people. He then ascended into heaven and sat down at the right hand of God, from whence He shall come again in power and great glory.

'He shall prolong His days …' The prophecy was most certainly fulfilled. We have a living Saviour. 'Therefore He is also able to save to the uttermost those who come to God through Him, since He ever lives to make intercession for them' (Hebrews 7:25).

Christ's resurrection—as we intimated earlier—is part of His state of exaltation which followed the humiliation of the cross. The Shorter Catechism states: 'Christ's exaltation consisteth in His rising again from the dead on the third day, in ascending up into heaven, in sitting at the right hand of God the Father, and in coming to judge the world at the last day'[1].

(c) Christ's Prosperity

'The pleasure of the LORD shall prosper in His hand.' The sufferings of Christ were supremely successful and not wasteful, for God's will prospered and flourished through them. Christ's death was certainly no waste of life, for the death of Christ accomplished the eternal salvation of God's elect. The Bible is clear that Christ died to actually procure our salvation, not merely to make salvation possible. 'Christ Jesus came into the world to *save* sinners' (1 Timothy 1:15, emphasis mine). Hebrews 9:12 tells of His actually having obtained (that is, securing) eternal redemption 'with His Own blood.' Here is a Saviour who really saves. Here is a Redeemer who really redeems. Here is precious blood which really atones. Here is a death that bestows eternal life. Christ's work of salvation at Calvary was a perfect and eternal one. The will of the Lord to save His people prospered in His hand. 'When He had by Himself purged our sins, sat down at the right hand of the Majesty on high' (Hebrews 1:3).

The Successful Saviour

And so we see the tremendous success of the work of Christ in procuring the salvation of 'a great multitude which no one could number' (Revelation 7:9). Isaiah predicted that Christ's work on the cross would be a successful work, giving the believer rest by His sorrow and life by His death. Isaiah's prediction came true and will yet come true …

Perhaps it was with the blessed outcome of progeny, prolongation and prosperity in mind, that the writer of the epistle to the Hebrews was able to inform us of the Lord Jesus' inner frame of heart and mind as He faced and endured His Calvary sufferings. Knowing the blessed outcome of His pain and suffering, Hebrews 12:2 says that 'Jesus … for the *joy* that was set before Him endured the cross, despising the shame, and has sat down at the right hand of the throne of God.'

A tender plant from the dry ground

Reflect on these points

1. Did Christ die to make salvation possible or actual? Give Scripture proof for your answer.
2. 'If Christ is not risen, your faith is futile; you are still in your sins!' (1 Corinthians 15:17). What does Paul mean here?
3. A non-Christian friend asks you, 'Do you think that Christ really did rise from the dead?' Is the evidence for Christ's resurrection compelling?

The success

The satisfaction

'He shall see the travail of His soul and be satisfied.'

Isaiah 53:11

In our previous chapter, we have just mentioned how 'Jesus … for the joy that was set before Him endured the cross …' (Hebrews 12:2). Part of this joy was surely the joy of knowing that a great multitude of souls would be saved by His pains. Matthew Henry says this of our title verse:

> [Christ] shall with the prospect of His sufferings have a prospect of fruit, and He shall be satisfied with the bargain. He shall see it when it is accomplished in the conversion and salvation of poor sinners. The salvation of souls is a great satisfaction to the Lord Jesus. He will reckon all His pains well bestowed, and Himself abundantly recompensed, if the many sons be by Him brought through grace to glory. Let Him have this, and He has enough …[1]

Isaiah thus foresaw that Christ would foresee that His death was not in vain. Premature death in this life is one of the harsher providences. It seems so perplexingly pointless, futile and tragic. Christ's death, though, was none of these. Christ's death was purposeful, not pointless and fruitful, not futile. Life was to result from His death and eternal gain was to ensue from His excruciating pain. A glorious reaping resulted from the painful sowing of Calvary. It resulted in a blessed harvest of saved souls, to the eternal glory of God the Father and the

A tender plant from the dry ground

eternal satisfaction of God the Son. 'He shall the travail of His soul and be satisfied.'

Specifically, Isaiah delineates here:

(A) Fruit

'... the *fruit* of the travail of His soul' (RSV, emphasis mine). Paradoxically, in the natural world, fruit is a result of death. As the apostle Paul wrote, 'What you sow is not made alive unless it dies' (1 Corinthians 15:36). The Saviour Himself uttered a similar sentiment. Speaking of His impending death as prophesied by Isaiah here, He explained: 'The hour has come that the Son of Man should be glorified. Most assuredly, I say to you, unless a grain of wheat falls into the ground and dies, it remains alone; but if it dies, it produces much grain' (John 12:23, 24).

In the natural realm, fruit is the result of the death of a seed. And it is the same in the spiritual realm. Fruit is the result of the death of the Saviour. Had the Saviour not died, there would have been no salvation, for the wages of sin would have gone unpaid, and so would have to be eternally paid by the sinner. But because the Saviour died, there is eternal hope. His death procured the eternal salvation of all who believe in Him. His death has resulted and will yet result in fruit—an immense harvest of souls of sinners saved by grace.

The Lord Jesus was evidently fond of the harvest metaphor as a depiction of both salvation and damnation. He told both the Parable of the Sower and the Parable of the Wheat and Tares. The latter climaxed with the pronouncement: 'Let both

The satisfaction

grow together until the harvest; and at the time of the harvest I will say to the reapers, 'First gather together the tares and bind them in bundles to burn them, but gather the wheat into my barn' (Matthew 13:30).

Secondly, we note that Isaiah specifically mentions:

(B) THE TRAVAIL OF HIS SOUL

'… the travail of His soul …' In line with the whole Bible, Isaiah is far more concerned with the spiritual sufferings of the Servant than His physical ones. Isaiah focuses on the travail of His *soul*—even though the suffering He was to experience in His body would be absolutely excruciating. Christ 'endured most grievous torments immediately in His soul, and most painful sufferings in His body; was crucified, and died, was buried …'[2]

Christ's pain, then, was a 'travail of soul'. The word 'travail' here is the word used of a woman's labour pains. Labour pains are some of the severest pains a woman will ever experience. Yet these pains have a happy outcome: the birth of a child and a new life in the world. In the physical world, a woman's labour pain leads to the joy of childbirth.

In the spiritual realm, the 'labour pains' of Christ, that is, the travail of His soul at Calvary, also resulted in new life—eternal life for all who believe. It was the travail of Christ's soul which wrought our salvation, and saves us from spiritual death.

The 'gain from pain' metaphor of labour pains and childbirth is a frequent one in the Bible. The Middle Eastern setting of the Bible was less inhibited about this somewhat delicate matter than perhaps we are in the west. Again though, with His death at Calvary impending, Jesus said to His disciples:

'A woman, when she is in labour has sorrow, because her hour has come; but as soon as she has given birth to the child, she no longer remembers the anguish, for joy that a human being has been born into the world. Therefore you now have sorrow, but I will see you again and your heart will rejoice, and your joy no one will take from you' (John 16:21, 22).

Hence a woman's travail, paradoxically, is a 'happy pain.' It results in new life. Christ's travail of soul may be viewed similarly. His death wrought our life. His pain wrought our pardon. His suffering wrought our salvation. His agony wrought our atonement. 'He shall see the fruit of the travail of His soul and be satisfied' (RSV).

Satisfied

Much in this fallen world is unsatisfactory. We are imperfect people and hence all we are and all we do fail to be perfectly satisfactory in one way or another. 'Room for improvement' and 'Could do better' is not confined solely to children's school reports!

The work of Christ at Calvary, however, was a perfect work. Nothing could be added to it by way of improvement, and nothing can ever be taken away from it. 'It is finished' (John 19:30). The perfect Saviour wrought a perfect salvation. By His work, 'God will be glorified, penitent believers will be justified and then Christ will be satisfied' (Mathew Henry).

The satisfaction

There is nothing dissatisfactory about the work of Christ on the cross.

Reflect on these points

1. *Crucifixion was a common occurrence in the Roman Empire of the first century. What is it that puts the crucifixion of Christ in an infinitely different category from other crucifixions?*
2. *'No pain, no gain.' Think of examples of this in the Bible. Think of examples of this from your own life.*
3. *'Every false way of salvation casts aspersions on the sufficiency of the finished work of Christ.' Is that statement true? Look up Galatians 2:21.*

The salvation

'By His knowledge My righteous Servant shall justify many ...'

Isaiah 53:11

The Gospel of Justification

'Justification'—that is, being 'accounted righteous' before God—is integral to the way in which the Bible understands salvation, and justification is therefore—according to Martin Luther—the mark of a standing or falling church. Justification is a most vital, biblical doctrine, thus a definition will be helpful before we continue. The Shorter Catechism defines justification thus:

> Justification is an act of God's free grace, wherein He pardoneth all our sins and accepteth us as righteous in His sight, only for the righteousness of Christ imputed to us, and received by faith alone. [1]

Roderick Lawson elucidates this further. Unpacking this concise statement for us, he comments:

> Justification means pronouncing a person righteous; it is the opposite of condemnation. It is said to be an act, because it is done at once; and an act of God's free grace, because we can do nothing of ourselves to deserve it. It consists of two parts—pardon and acceptance; and we are taught also that the cause of it is not our own goodness, but Christ's, and that Christ's righteousness becomes ours through faith. [2]

Here, then, is the 'Gospel according to Isaiah.' Isaiah proclaims and exclaims that 'by His knowledge', that is, by knowing, trusting and cleaving to God's 'righteous Servant' many shall be 'justified', that is, accounted righteous. By trusting in the Christ to come, and His work on behalf of sinners, says Isaiah, many shall be justified, that is, guilty sinners would be acquitted and declared 'not guilty' in God's sight. The unrighteous would be delivered from condemnation and declared righteous because of the merits of Christ, the righteous One. The ill-deserving and hell-deserving would enjoy the blessing of God's salvation. Truly, when we consider the holiness of God and the terror and plight of having to face Him in our natural, sinful state, the gospel according to Isaiah is good news indeed. Salvation means deliverance. Justification means being acquitted. The message of the Bible and the message of Isaiah 53 is that 'There is therefore now no condemnation to those who are in Christ Jesus' (Romans 8:1).

God's way of Justification

The question is begged as to whether Isaiah's gospel is too good to be true? Can guilty sinners really be acquitted in God's sight? If they can, does this not compromise the justice which is integral to God's being?

The gospel of justification is not man's gospel but God's. He alone could solve the dilemma and seeming conflict between the love and justice which is part of His nature. He alone could 'demonstrate at the present time His righteousness, that He might be just and the justifier of the one who has faith in Jesus' (Romans 3:26).

Were God to acquit sinners, His justice would be compromised, for no infraction of His Law can be left unpaid. Were God to condemn all sinners, we would know nothing of His grace and mercy. The answer and resolution to this divine dilemma is the suffering Servant foretold by Isaiah—the Christ of Calvary. Calvary is the supreme manifestation of both the love and justice of God. In the substitutionary death of Christ at Calvary, God both condemned sin (satisfying His justice) and pardoned the sinner (revealing His mercy). Paradoxically, at the cross we see both the love and the wrath of God. 'In this is love, not that we loved God but that He loved us and sent His Son to be the propitiation for our sins' (1 John 4:10). As the Psalmist also foretold: 'Mercy and truth have met together; Righteousness and peace have kissed each other' (Psalm 85:10).

Isaiah's matchless prophecy is thus all apiece. His gospel of justification is inseparable from the Servant's substitutionary death—that is, that He was to serve the sentence owed to sinners. 'He shall bear their iniquities'(Isaiah 53:11). Christ was judged that we might be justified. He was condemned that we might be acquitted. 'For He made Him who knew no sin to be sin for us, that we might become the righteousness of God in Him' (2 Corinthians 5:21).

God's acquittal, then, flows to sinners because the sinless, righteous One bore their punishment in their room and stead, so that by believing in Him—'knowing Him'—we may go free. As a compass always points north, we return again to Isaiah's central stanza, and remind ourselves that our being accounted righteous in God's sight is due solely to one fact: 'He was wounded for our transgressions, He was bruised for our iniquities; the chastisement for our peace was upon Him, and by His stripes we are healed' (Isaiah 53:5).

Isaiah's gospel, then, is a gospel of justification. The evangelical prophet declares that 'by His knowledge My righteous Servant shall justify many'. Similarly, in Isaiah 61:10 the prophet exuberates in words which every justified sinner can make their own: 'I will greatly rejoice in the Lord, my soul shall be joyful in my God; for He has clothed me with the garments of salvation, He has covered me with the robe of righteousness.'

The Gospel of the Bible

It is well known that the gospel of justification came to the forefront at the time of the Protestant Reformation. The Protestant Reformation cannot be separated from Martin Luther's discovery—or rediscovery—of the gospel of God's justifying grace. It was Luther's study of Paul's letter to the Romans which led to Luther's salvation. Initially he tried to work arduously to get right with God his Maker. But then the Holy Spirit revealed the gospel of justification to him, through the Word, that 'to him who does not work but believes on Him Who justifies the ungodly, his faith is accounted for righteousness' (Romans 4:5). Luther thus did not invent the gospel of justification; rather he recovered the gospel of justification from Paul. Paul himself did not invent the gospel of justification either. Rather, Paul in Romans was just giving a detailed exposition of what the Saviour Himself had already taught. The Lord Jesus once told a parable about a good man who went to hell and a bad man who went to heaven. The bad man went to heaven solely because of the mercy of God. The 'good' man—like Luther before his conversion—aspired to being a self-righteous man. His gospel was 'justification by respectability'. He was badly and sadly mistaken. His righteousness, although admirable in the sight of men, was not good enough in the sight of God. His good works were not sufficient to save him. The bad man, though, confessed his sinfulness and cast himself on God's mercy. 'God be merciful to me a sinner!' (Luke 18:13). Jesus concluded the parable by proclaiming: 'I tell you, this man' (that is the 'bad man') 'went down to his house justified rather than the other …' (Luke 18:14).

Isaiah's Gospel

Isaiah's gospel of justification, then, is the gospel of the Bible. There is only one gospel—'the gospel of God' (Romans 1:1) —the gospel of God's justification of guilty sinners by virtue of the suffering which Christ endured in their place. If we are truly trusting in Him, we are justified for time and eternity! 'By His knowledge shall My righteous Servant justify many' (Isaiah 53:11). The Christian alone can joyfully lay down the challenge: 'Who shall bring a charge against God's elect? It is God Who justifies. Who is he who condemns?' (Romans 8:33, 34). Isaiah's gospel of justification is good news indeed.

Reflect on these points

1. *Justification is not the only New Testament metaphor for salvation, yet it is central to the Reformed understanding of salvation. Memorise the Shorter Catechism's definition of justification.*
2. *Consider the words of Article XI of the 'Thirty-nine Articles of the Church of England': 'We are accounted righteous before God only for the merit of our Lord and Saviour Jesus Christ by faith, and not for our own works or deservings: Wherefore, that we are justified by faith only is a most wholesome doctrine, and very full of comfort.'*
3. *A Christian's eternal confidence rests on the imputed righteousness of Christ. Is self-righteousness the distinguishing mark of every non-Christian religion?*

The salvation

The sin-bearer

'... *for He shall bear their iniquities.*'

Isaiah 53:11

In his book *The Story of the Church*, the late Professor A. M. Renwick relates the conversion of Charles Simeon—an influential Anglican evangelical minister in Cambridge in the eighteenth century—in these words:

> A young man of intense sincerity, Simeon soon awakened to the need of putting himself right with God, and made the momentous discovery, in his own words, that he could transfer his guilt to another. 'I sought,' he wrote, 'to lay my sins on the sacred head of Jesus.'[1]

Christ as 'sin-bearer' is what our verse above is all about. Sin and guilt is the most heavy, grievous and damnable burden that we fallen human beings can carry. The Psalmist confessed, 'For my iniquities have gone over my head; Like a heavy burden they are too heavy for me' (Psalm 38:4). But Isaiah gladly prophesied One who would relieve and release this burden from off His people. 'He shall bear their iniquities.' Yet again, only one Person fits Isaiah's prophetic description and depiction: the Christ of Calvary.

The Bearer of Sin

Isaiah prophesied that the coming Servant would be a bearer of sin—and sin not His own—no fewer than three times in his famous prophecy:

> v.6: 'and the LORD has laid on Him the iniquity of us all.'
>
> v.11: 'for He shall bear their iniquities.'
>
> v.12: 'He bore the sin of many.'

That these prophesies were fulfilled in Christ is both the implicit and explicit testimony of the New Testament. Pointing to Christ, John the Baptist proclaimed, 'Behold! The Lamb of God who takes away the sin of the world' (John 1:29). Peter—a disciple who was initially somewhat puzzled and confused by Christ's cross—wrote with the benefit of hindsight in 1 Peter 2:24: 'Who Himself bore our sins in His own body on the tree.' John also explained in 1 John 3:5 that 'You know that He was manifested to take away sins, and in Him there is no sin.'

Christ as sin-bearer, then, is central to both Isaiah's prophecy and to a true understanding of His Calvary work. But what exactly does the Bible mean when it speaks of Christ in terms of being a sin-bearer? Let us allow the late John R.W. Stott to explain:

> The expression to 'bear sin' has a rather foreign sound in our ears, and we shall need to go back to the Old Testament to understand it. The idea occurs frequently in the books of Leviticus and Numbers ... For instance, 'If any one sins, doing any of the things which the LORD has commanded not to be done ... he is guilty and shall bear his iniquity' (Leviticus 5:19). The expression

The sin-bearer

can only mean one thing. To 'bear sin' is to suffer the consequences of one's sin, to bear its penalty.

But at times it is implied that somebody else can assume responsibility for the sinner ...

This possibility of somebody else accepting the responsibility for, and bearing the consequences of, our sins was further taught by those Old Testament blood sacrifices in the Mosaic legislation. Of the sin offering it was said that God had given it to 'bear the iniquity of the congregation, to make atonement for them before the LORD' (Leviticus 10:17). It is plain from this that to 'bear' somebody else's sin is to become his substitute, to bear the penalty of his sin in his place.

The Son of God identified Himself with the sins of men. He was not content to take our nature upon Him; He took our iniquity upon Him as well. He was not only 'made flesh' in the womb of Mary; He was 'made sin' on the cross of Calvary ...[2]

Christ, then, is the Saviour who takes our sin and guilt away. He took it away when He suffered its consequences at Calvary. We cannot escape from the central affirmation of the New Testament in general, and Isaiah's fifty-third chapter in particular, that Christ is the substitutionary, sin-bearer. 'He was wounded for our transgressions...' If we take this away, we have no gospel to proclaim. The gospel of Isaiah, and the gospel of the Bible says that **G**od's **O**wn **S**on **P**aid **E**very

A tender plant from the dry ground

Liability—GOSPEL. Taken up with the greatness of the gospel of reconciliation, the apostle Paul in 2 Corinthians 5:19 states that 'God was in Christ reconciling the world to Himself, not imputing their trespasses to them' (2 Corinthians 5:19). It is good to know for, as the Psalmist said: 'If You, LORD, should mark iniquities, O Lord, who could stand?' (Psalm 130:3). This blessed 'not counting' or 'non-imputation' of our trespasses is only possible because they were counted or imputed to Another. They were imputed to the sin-bearer, the Lord Jesus Christ. On the cross He bore them away in His sinless body. Paul climaxes 2 Corinthians 5 with the stupendous assertion: 'For He made Him who knew no sin to be sin for us, so that we might become the righteousness of God in Him' (2 Corinthians 5:21). That Christ really does take away the burden of our sin and condemnation is the personal experience and testimony uniting all true Christians, irrespective of nationality or denomination. All are one at the foot of the cross. Christ is a Saviour who really saves!

The Great Burden Bearer

Isaiah thus foretold of One who would bear the burden of our sins. 'He shall bear their iniquities.' He thus foretold of the Christ to come. Today, the Saviour still invites sinners to unburden their burden of sin on Him. His invitation still avails: 'Come to Me all you who labour and are heavy laden, and I will give you rest' (Matthew 11:28). It is a crucial matter, for if our sins have not been borne by the sin-bearing Saviour, we will bear them and their damnation ourselves—and we will do so eternally. Isaiah's prophecy of the sin-bearer is therefore both good news to receive and a gospel to proclaim, and proclaim with urgency.

Reflect on these points

1. *What exactly does a Christian mean when he or she states 'Jesus bore my sins.'?*
2. *What are the consequences of not knowing Christ as our sin-bearer? And what are the practical implications of this?*
3. *Is it really possible for one person to take the liability for the sins of all God's elect?*
4. *Is a Christian's assurance of salvation presumption, or is it normal, New Testament Christianity?*

The song

'Therefore I will divide Him a portion with the great, and He shall divide the spoil with the strong; because He poured out His soul unto death, and He was numbered with the transgressors ...'

Isaiah 53:12

Isaiah's prophecy concerning the Suffering Servant who was to come has now gone full circle. His first and last verses in this matchless prophecy coalesce. Isaiah began with the Servant's exaltation—'Behold, My Servant shall deal prudently; He shall be exalted and extolled and be very high' (Isaiah 52:13)—and now ends similarly on an exalted note, with the Servant's glorification: 'Therefore I will divide Him a portion with the great, and He shall divide the spoil with the strong.' Note well the reason for the Servant's glorification, though. It was because He did everything needful and necessary for the salvation of His people. He was glorified 'because He poured out His soul to death, and He was numbered with the transgressors.' As T. T. Shields well said, 'The death of the Lord Jesus is the ground of His supremest glory.'[1] 'We see Jesus ... for the suffering of death crowned with glory and honour, that He, by the grace of God might taste death for everyone' (Hebrews 2:9).

The apostle Peter wrote that the prophets predicted both 'the sufferings of Christ and the glories that would follow' (1 Peter 1:10, 11). In our title verse we are dealing with 'the glories that would follow': 'Therefore I will divide Him a portion with the great, and He shall divide the spoil with the

A tender plant from the dry ground

strong.' Were we to take an 'impressionist' view of this verse, as opposed to an analytical one, we would say that it has a celebratory feel to it. It is speaking exuberantly of a victory after a battle. It is speaking of and celebrating a glorious conquest.

Let us now analyse the verse a little more closely:

(A) 'THEREFORE I WILL DIVIDE HIM A PORTION WITH THE GREAT ...'

The Servant is here receiving the honour which is His due because of His redeeming work. The Holy Spirit is employing the language of earth to depict something of the Servant's heavenly exaltation. 'God will reward His Servant as if He was a king sharing in the spoils of a great victory.'[2] It is interesting to note that here, God the Son is being honoured by God the Father because of His accomplished work of redemption. An early Christian hymn describes the same phenomenon, when it says that God the Son 'humbled Himself and became obedient to the point of death, even the death of the cross,' and, 'Therefore God [the Father] also has highly exalted Him and given Him the name which is above every name' (Philippians 2:8, 9). It is as though Isaiah is depicting Christ as the honoured head of a feast, and His special guests are those whom He has redeemed. Interestingly, the last book of the Bible depicts the culmination and climax of salvation as a glorious feast: 'Blessed are those who are called to the marriage supper of the Lamb' (Revelation 19:9). Christ the Saviour will certainly be the honoured Head and Host of this Feast in the coming day of salvation's consummation.

(B) 'AND HE SHALL DIVIDE THE SPOIL WITH THE STRONG ...'

'Dividing the spoil' is a metaphor which speaks of a victory after a battle. Isaiah had previously said, in another Messianic prophecy, how 'men rejoice when they divide the spoil' (Isaiah 9:3). 'Spoil' here refers to the plunder taken from an enemy city after its capture and defeat. Isaiah is prophesying that the Saviour to come would be a victorious Saviour. Jesus Himself viewed His ministry in similar terms too, for He spoke of Himself as a Strong Man, binding a strong man (Satan) and then plundering his goods: 'When a strong man, fully armed, guards his own palace, his goods are in peace; but when a stronger than he comes upon him and overcomes him, he takes from him all his armour in which he trusted, and divides his spoil,' (Luke 11:21, 22).

The Christ of the Bible was victorious in His mission, and He shares His victory with God's elect. Jesus gained a complete victory over sin, death and Satan, and shares the benefits of this victory with all who believe in Him. 'Death is swallowed up in victory ... thanks be to God, who gives us the victory through our Lord Jesus Christ' (1 Corinthians 15:54, 57). 'Having disarmed principalities and powers, He made a public spectacle of them, triumphing over them in [the cross]' (Colossians 2:15) ... that through death He might destroy him who has the power of death, that is, the devil (Hebrews 2:14). The Christ of the Bible is a victorious, conquering Christ, infinitely worthy of an honoured victory celebration.

A tender plant from the dry ground

The Victory Song

In the Bible, singing accompanies and is a consequence of salvation, hence the title of this chapter concerning Christ's glory and conquest. The fact that He shares His glory and victory with sinners is a cause of celebration. He conquered by His cross, and believers in Him 'are more than conquerors through Him who loved us' (Romans 8:37). The salvation which Christ secured for us at Calvary is fuel for our heartfelt praise. Joyful song is a consequence of divine salvation:

When the Lord finally delivered His people from bondage in Egypt, 'Moses and the people sang this song to the LORD, and spoke, saying 'I will sing to the LORD, for He has triumphed gloriously …' (Exodus 15:1).

When the Lord delivered the Psalmist 'up out of a horrible pit, out of the miry clay, and set my feet upon a rock', he relates that consequentially 'He has put a new song in my mouth—Praise to our God' (Psalm 40:3).

There is, says the Lord Jesus, 'joy in the presence of the angels of God over one sinner who repents' (Luke 15:10).

And the heavenly chorus is and will for ever be the song of the Christian. In heaven they sing the song of salvation—a salvation accomplished at Calvary, enjoyed now on earth, but consummated in glory: 'they sang a new song … saying "Worthy is the Lamb who was slain"' (Revelation 5:12) … 'You were slain, and have redeemed us to God by Your blood …' (Revelation 5:9). Christians alone have reason to sing, for Christians alone have a salvation worth celebrating and a Saviour worth praising.

The song

Reflect on these points

1. Consider this statement: 'The chief task of the church is divine worship.'
2. 'Christians have a salvation worth celebrating.' How much true Christian joy and celebration have you known in the last seven days? How are the fires of Christian joy and devotion maintained?
3. Does the Christian faith involve a salvation anticipated in the future, as well as a salvation enjoyed in the present? How does the Christian's future hope affect life in the here and now?

The service

'Because He poured out His soul unto death, and was numbered with the transgressors, and He bore the sin of many, and made intercession for the transgressors'

Isaiah 53:1

Isaiah closes and concludes his marvellous, matchless prophecy concerning the Suffering Servant to come, by drawing our attention to another facet of the service He would give. Particularly, he draws our attention to the Servant's priestly ministry. In Old Testament times, a priest's service comprised two tasks: (a) Offering sacrifice for sin and (b) Making intercession for sinners. In this final verse, Isaiah notes that the Servant to come would undertake both of these duties. Speaking in the prophetic past tense, he states that Christ: (a) 'bore the sin of many' (sacrifice) and (b) 'made intercession for the transgressors' (intercession). Isaiah thus foresaw that part of the service which the Servant to come would give would be that of the service of a priest.

Our Great High Priest

That the Priest of whom Isaiah spoke found its fulfilment and culmination in the ministry of the Lord Jesus Christ, is the unanimous witness of the New Testament in general and the epistle to the Hebrews in particular. 'Seeing then that we have a great high priest who has passed through the heavens, Jesus, the Son of God, let us hold fast our confession' (Hebrews 4:14).

Christ's office of priest is another aspect of His being the

Messiah. As Messiah, Christ combines and fulfils the threefold office of prophet, priest and king in His one divine Person. In the words of the Shorter Catechism, 'Christ as our Redeemer, executeth the offices of a prophet, of a *priest* and of a king, both in His estate of humiliation and exaltation'.[1]

Our verse, with its attention given to Christ's sacrifice and intercession, draws our minds to Christ's office of priest. 'He bore the sin of many, and made intercession for the transgressors.'

In answer to the question 'How doth Christ execute the office of a priest?', the *Shorter Catechism* states: 'Christ executeth the office of a priest in His once offering up of Himself a sacrifice, to satisfy divine justice, and reconcile us to God; and in making continual intercession for us.'[2]

Lawson's comment on this elucidates:

> The duties of a priest were to offer sacrifices and pray for the people; and this is what Christ, as our priest, does for us. When He was here on earth, He offered Himself as a sacrifice; and now that He is in heaven, He intercedes for us with the Father.[3]

We will thus now consider finally: (a) Christ's sacrifice—His finished work and (b) Christ's intercession—His continuing work.

(A) THE PRIESTLY SACRIFICE OF CHRIST

'He poured out His soul unto death … He bore the sin of many …'

The service

Sacrifice was a central part of a priest's duties under the Mosaic law. 'For every high priest taken from among men is appointed for men in things pertaining to God, that he may offer both gifts and sacrifices for sins' (Hebrews 5:1). Sacrifice—as we saw in a previous chapter—spoke both of the holiness of God and the seriousness of sin. The sinner deserved to die, but in His mercy, God ordained that an innocent animal could die in the sinner's place, foreshadowing the Great Sacrifice that was yet to come and bring full salvation. In this sense, the slain animal was a substitutionary sacrifice.

When Isaiah foresaw the Priest who was to come, He noted that the sacrifice He would offer would not be an animal, but would actually be His own sinless life. 'He makes Himself an offering for sin' (Isaiah 53:10) … 'He poured out His soul unto death' (Isaiah 53:12). Here, then, is no ordinary sacrifice. Here is a special sacrifice. Here is a sacrifice which is mighty to save. And the unanimous testimony of both the New Testament and of all Christ's redeemed people, is that Christ's sacrifice of Himself at Calvary is a sacrifice sufficient to save the believing soul for all eternity. The sacrifice of Christ was a perfect sacrifice. Nothing can be added to it and nothing can be taken from it. Those availing themselves of it receive eternal atonement for their sins, for the sacrifice of Calvary was nothing less than the sacrifice of the eternal Son of God. 'But now, once at the end of the ages, He has appeared to put away sin by the sacrifice of Himself' (Hebrews 9:26). This sacrifice fulfils all the Old Testament sacrifices and renders all sacrifice obsolete.

'Who does not need daily, as those high priests, to offer up sacrifice, first for his own sins and then the people's, for this He did once for all when He offered up Himself' (Hebrews 7:27). The Christian's rallying cry thus is 'No priest but Christ' and 'No sacrifice but Calvary'.

(b) The Priestly Supplication of Christ

'He … made intercession for the transgressors.'

When Christ was nailed to the cross, He interceded for His persecutors, rather than crying out in vengeance to God to judge them. 'And when they come to the place called Calvary, there they crucified Him … Then Jesus said, "Father, forgive them; for they do not know what they do"' (Luke 23:33, 34). Matthew Henry comments:

> He prayed 'Father, forgive them,' thereby showing, not only that He forgave them, but that He was now doing that upon which their forgiveness, and the forgiveness of all other transgressors, were to be founded'.[4]

Our Heavenly Intercessor

'He … made intercession for the transgressors.'

The New Testament teaches that Christ's intercession is a work which He still does. As Aaron, the high priest in Moses' day, bore the names of the children of Israel on both his shoulders and his heart before God (see Exodus 28), how much more does Christ bear those for whom He died before God the Father. Christ is a High Priest in heaven who continues to intercede for His own. 'Christ … died … is also risen, who is even at the right hand of God, who also makes intercession for us …' (Romans 8:34). 'He is also able to save to the uttermost those who come to God through Him, since He ever lives to make intercession for them' (Hebrews 7:25).

The continual intercession of Christ for His own is possibly a neglected aspect of His ministry. Christ's continual intercession for His own, though, is a New Testament fact of immense comfort to the Christian. Christ intervened to save us by dying, and He still intervenes on our behalf by interceding. He pleads our case before the throne of God. He pleads our case, not on the basis of who we are, but on the basis of what He has done. The nail prints in His hands and the wound in His side are a continual reminder to the Father that He has dealt with our sins. 'Christ has entered … into heaven itself, now to appear in the presence of God for us' (Hebrews 9:24). Writing to Christians, John states, 'If any one sins, we have an Advocate with the Father, Jesus Christ the righteous' (1 John 2:1). The ground of the believer's eternal security is the one sacrifice which Christ made on our behalf and His continual work of intercession on our behalf. Transgressions against God's law deserve punishment for sure, 'But He was wounded for our transgressions … and made intercession for the transgressors.'

Christ, our great High Priest, therefore made intercession and still makes intercession for sinners like us. Let us allow James Packer to sum up what we have just stated concerning the comforting truth of the heavenly intercession of our heavenly Saviour:

> We should define Christ's intercession as that heavenly activity ... whereby He makes sure that all who come to God through Him, pleading His Name, trusting Him for forgiveness, access, grace to help in time of need, and ultimate glory, will not be disappointed.[5]

Conclusion

On that encouraging note, we take our leave of our reflections on Isaiah's superlative prophecy. His famous fifty-third chapter is a prophecy which concerns the Lord Jesus Christ in all the glory of His Person and in all the efficacy of His saving work for sinners. The 'Gospel according to Isaiah' is the gospel of our Lord and Saviour Jesus Christ. There is no other gospel. Christ alone is the answer to our every need, to His eternal glory and praise.

The service

Reflect on these points
1. *What were the chief tasks of an Old Testament priest? How are these tasks fulfilled in Christ?*
2. *What do we mean by (a) The finished work of Christ. (b) The continuing work of Christ? Is there a connection between the two? (See 1 John 2:1,2).*
3. *'With Isaiah 53, it is a matter of history interpreting prophecy and prophecy interpreting history.' Explain this statement in your own words.*
4. *In what ways have your appreciation of Christ and your wonder at the Word of God increased through these reflections on Isaiah 53?*

Soli Deo Gloria

A tender plant from the dry ground

Endnotes

Ch. 1 The surprise
   1 *The Westminster Shorter Catechism*, Question 31
   2 *The Westminster Shorter Catechism*

Ch. 3 The shape
   1 *Day by Day: Moments with the Master*, C.E. Hocking, Gospel Folio Press, p.36
   2 Te Deum, *The Book of Common Prayer*

Ch. 5 The sorrow
   1 *The Westminster Shorter Catechism*, Questions 21 and 22
   2 Matthew Henry, *A commentary on the whole Bible*, p.237

Ch. 6 The substitute
   1 *Evangelical Times*, Darlington, England, January 2003, p.21

Ch. 8 The silence
   1 Louis Berkhof, *Systematic Theology*, Banner of Truth Trust, p.381
   2 John Ellerton, *Silent through those three dread hours*

Ch. 12 The sinlessness
   1 Philip P Bliss, Man of Sorrows! what a name

Ch. 13 The sovereignty
   1 *The Westminster Shorter Catechism*, Question 7

Ch. 14 The sacrifice
   1 *The Lion Encyclopaedia of the Bible*, p. 127
   2 Not all the blood of beasts, Isaac Watts
   3 This phrase is from *The Book of Common Prayer*

Endnotes

Ch. 15 The success
1. *The Westminster Shorter Catechism*, Question 28

Ch. 16 The satisfaction
1. Matthew Henry, *A commentary on the whole Bible*, Volume 4, p.242
2. *The Westminster Confession of Faith*, Chapter 8, paragraph 4

Ch. 17 The salvation
1. *The Westminster Shorter Catechism*, Question 33
2. Rev Roderick Lawson, *The Shorter Catechism with commentary, proofs and revising questions*, Maybole, Published by the Sabbath School Society for Ireland, Belfast, p. 25

Ch. 18 The sin-bearer
1. *The Story of the Church*, Alexander Renwick, IVP, p.169
2. John R W Stott, *Basic Christianity*, IVP, pp.90, 91, 92

Ch. 19 The song
1. T T Shields, *Sermons on Isaiah 53*, p.147
2. *The NIV Study Bible*, p.1077

Ch. 20 The song
1. *The Westminster Shorter Catechism*, Question 23
2. Ibid, Question 25
3. Roderick Lawson, *Shorter Catechism*, op cit
4. Matthew Henry, *A commentary on the whole Bible*, Vol. 4, p.241
5. James I Packer, *God's Words*, p. 118

About Day One:

Day One's threefold commitment:
- To be faithful to the Bible, God's inerrant, infallible Word;
- To be relevant to our modern generation;
- To be excellent in our publication standards.

I continue to be thankful for the publications of Day One. They are biblical; they have sound theology; and they are relevant to the issues at hand. The material is condensed and manageable while, at the same time, being complete—a challenging balance to find. We are happy in our ministry to make use of these excellent publications.
JOHN MACARTHUR, PASTOR-TEACHER, GRACE COMMUNITY CHURCH, CALIFORNIA

It is a great encouragement to see Day One making such excellent progress. Their publications are always biblical, accessible and attractively produced, with no compromise on quality. Long may their progress continue and increase!
JOHN BLANCHARD, AUTHOR, EVANGELIST AND APOLOGIST

Visit our web site for more information and to request a free catalogue of our books.
www.dayone.co.uk

U.S. web site:
www.dayonebookstore.com